clay POT
COOKING

clay POT
COOKING

THE PERFECT WAY TO COOK ALMOST ANYTHING

KATHRYN HAWKINS

CHARTWELL
BOOKS, INC.

A QUINTET BOOK

Published by Chartwell Books
A Division of Book Sales, Inc.
114, Northfield Avenue
Edison, New Jersey 08837

This edition produced for sale in the U.S.A., its territories and dependencies only.

ISBN 0-7858-0911-2

This book was designed and produced by
Quintet Publishing Limited
6 Blundell Street
London N7 9BH

Creative Director: Richard Dewing
Art Director: Clare Reynolds
Designer: Caroline Grimshaw
Senior Editor: Laura Sandelson
Photographer: Janine Hosegood
Home Economist: Sally Mansfield

Typeset in Great Britain by
Central Southern Typesetters, Eastbourne
Manufactured in Singapore by
Eray Scan Pte Ltd
Printed in Singapore by
Star Standard Industries Pte. Ltd.

Acknowledgements
The Publishers would like to thank Life File for supplying the
pictures on pages 6 and 9 (bottom), and David Mellor of Sloane Square, SW1 for supplying
the claypots appearing on pages 7 (left), 8 (right), and 9 left.

contents

introduction

Cooking in a claypot has been in practice for hundreds of years, dating as far back as the Romans, and it continues to be widely used today all over the world. The Greeks cook their famous lamb dish, Kleftiko, in a clay baker, the French have their delicious pot roasts, and Indian Tandoori dishes are also cooked by this method. The resulting food is tender and flavorful.

A claypot is a very versatile cooking utensil, enabling you to roast and pot roast, cook casseroles and soups, and even bake puddings, cakes, and breads.

Before cooking can begin, the pot must be soaked in cold water. The terracotta absorbs moisture which helps to create the right enclosed environment for this unique cooking method. The food is kept moist, you do not need to add any fat, and basting is unnecessary during cooking. All the flavors are kept in, giving you the tastiest dishes ever, with the minimum amount of effort. There are a few tips you need to know before you begin, so read on and then enjoy the delights of claypot cooking for yourself.

WOMEN SELLING CLAYPOTS IN OUED-LAOU MARKET, MOROCCO

UNGLAZED EARTHENWARE POT

UNGLAZED TERRACOTTA SCHLEMMER-TOPF®

Hints and tips on claypot cooking

It is important to follow the manufacturer's instructions to prevent damage and to ensure success. If your claypot is new, wash it in hot water with a little liquid detergent, and then rinse thoroughly.

Before cooking, always soak the pot and lid in cold water for at least 15 minutes – if the claypot has not been used before, increase the soaking time to 30 minutes. Immerse completely in the water – the sink or a bowl is the best vessel for this. During soaking, the terracotta absorbs moisture and this is released as the pot is heated in the oven, thus creating a moist cooking atmosphere.

Drain from the water, and the pot is ready to use. Cooking results from the claypot will be tender and flavorful. You will find that cakes and baked dishes will rise well.

For some baking you will need to line the base of the claypot with waxed paper. This will ensure that baked goods are easy to remove.

If you are using your pot for the first time, and want to use it for a wide variety of foods, avoid cooking fish or seafood the first time. Once you have cooked other foods, then the claypot can be used for fish and seafood. This will avoid tainting other foods, especially desserts, with this flavor.

Cooking temperature

Never expose a claypot to any sudden change in temperature, as this will result in cracking and breakage.

The claypot must be placed in a cold oven and heated gradually. Set the temperature once the pot is inside and before increasing to the desired temperature. Never place in a preheated oven.

A very hot oven is needed for best results – 400° upward – this enables the retained moisture to evaporate.

Do not place a claypot directly onto the stove, or under a broiler.

Do not pour very hot or very cold liquid into the pot – it should be hand-hot; never place your claypot in the freezer.

During and after cooking

Once the pot is in the oven and the temperature is set, the food will require little or no attention – basting is unnecessary because the moisture evaporating from the pot will keep the food moist.

Arranging food in the claypot in a certain way will ensure that maximum flavor is maintained. Herbs and whole spices should be placed underneath meat, or pushed into vegetables, to enable their flavors to penetrate the food.

Because claypot cooking is a moist method of cooking, only a certain amount of browning takes place. Some recipes will suggest removing the lid just before the end of cooking to give a browner, "drier," crisper result. This applies to baked dishes with a topping: removing the lid will enable the top to crisp up before serving. Because the oven temperature is so hot, this final stage will only take a few minutes.

STONEWARE GARLIC BAKER

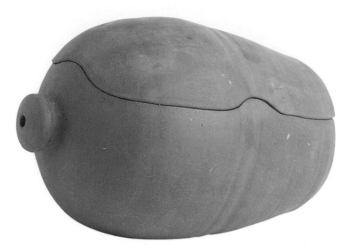

UNGLAZED EARTHENWARE TERRACOTTA CHICKEN BRICK

After cooking, care must be taken when you remove the pot from the oven. Place a wooden board, mat, or stand nearby, or a folded dish towel. Put the hot claypot on the prepared surface directly it comes out of the oven – never place the pot on a cold or wet surface. When you remove the lid, this will also need to be placed on a prepared surface.

To keep preparation to a minimum, you can serve straight from the claypot: just remember to place it on a heatproof mat on the table.

Microwave cooking

Claypots are suitable for microwave cooking, but a smaller one will probably be required in order to fit inside the oven. Soak the pot as you would for conventional cooking.

During microwave cooking, the pot absorbs microwave energy and will become hotter than other cookware. However, it cooks food more evenly, and ensures tender results.

Always follow the manufacturer's instructions for microwave temperature guidelines as these will vary from model to model. If you are adapting recipes, remember that cooking will be slower. The pot is usually used on a full-power setting (100%), but can be used on medium/high (70%) and medium (50%).

For combination microwave cooking, it is important not to preheat the oven. Once again, refer to the manufacturer's instructions, and remember to keep checking the food until you have become more familiar with the change in timings.

Cleaning

As time goes on, and you use your claypot more, you will notice that the pot changes color. It becomes "seasoned" like a wok or wooden salad bowl, and builds up its own protective layer. For this reason, avoid using detergents or abrasive cleaning materials, as these will damage the porous nature of the terracotta.

Always read the manufacturer's guidelines to see if your claypot is suitable to use in the dishwasher. If it is, rinse the claypot while still hot under very hot water to wash out any food residue or, if it is cold, rinse with cold water before placing in the dishwasher.

For hand washing, wash promptly after use in hot water using a mild detergent. Use only a washing-up brush gently to scrub off any residue; allow to soak if the residue is more stubborn. Rinse well in clean hot water and allow to drain. Allow to dry completely before storing.

If food is baked onto the claypot or the pot is heavily stained, it can be soaked overnight in very hot water and baking soda. This will also remove any unwanted flavors from the pot. Heavily tainted pots can be soaked as above, then rinsed and then filled with cold water, more baking soda, and a little detergent. Place in a cold oven and set the oven to 350°. Leave for 30 minutes. Increase to 450° and leave for a further 50 minutes. Remove from the oven and stand for 15 minutes. Then scrub the inside of the pot gently and pour away the water. Rinse in very hot water and allow to dry.

TERRACOTTA TANDOOR POT

EARTHENWARE BEAN POT

Storage

Once the claypot is completely dry, invert the lid in the pot and place in a cool dry closet. If the pot or conditions are damp during storage, the terracotta will be susceptible to mildew. If the lid is placed on the pot as for baking, this can lead to breakage. If the pot has not been used for a while or if storage conditions have been less than perfect, it is always advisable to wash the pot thoroughly before using.

Adapting recipes

Once you have mastered the art of claypot cooking, you will be able to adapt your favorite recipes by this method. Most claypot dishes are cooked at a much higher temperature than traditional recipes, but this is compensated for by the insulated protection from the pot itself. Take a look through the large selection of recipes in this book, and you should be able to use them to help you convert your own dishes into delicious claypot creations.

NOTE THE TAGINES FOR SALE AT THIS POTTERY MARKET NEAR AGADIR, MOROCCO.

soups

smoked sausage and lentil soup

A delicious smoked soup full of hearty ingredients to warm you on the coldest of days. Green lentils add a coarser texture, but if preferred you can substitute red lentils.

⬦

12 oz frankfurter sausages, sliced into 1-inch pieces
1 large onion, peeled and chopped
1 large red bell pepper, deseeded and sliced
1 large yellow bell pepper, deseeded and sliced
1 garlic clove, peeled and minced
1 tsp ground nutmeg
1 cup green lentils, rinsed in cold water
salt and black pepper
1½ quarts fresh vegetable broth, cooled
8 oz green cabbage, shredded
4 slices French bread
1 garlic clove, peeled and halved
4 Tbsp finely grated smoked cheese

⬦

PREPARATION TIME / **10 MINUTES**
COOKING TIME / **2 HOURS**
serves 4

Presoak the claypot as directed. Place the sausages, onion, bell peppers, garlic, nutmeg, and lentils in the pot and mix well. Season and pour over the broth. Cover and place in a cold oven. Set the oven to 400° and cook for 1½ hours. Stir in the cabbage, cover, and cook for a further 30 minutes.

To serve, preheat the broiler to a hot setting, and toast the bread for a few seconds on each side until golden. While the bread is still hot, rub the cut side of the garlic over the toast so it absorbs the flavor. Ladle the soup into warmed bowls and serve topped with a slice of the garlic bread and sprinkled with a little smoked cheese.

NUTRITION FACTS	
Serving size 1 (685g)	
Calories 518 Calories from fat 261	
	% daily value*
Total fat 29g	44%
Saturated fat 10g	52%
Cholesterol 75mg	25%
Sodium 1569mg	65%
Total carbohydrate 39g	13%
Dietary fiber 5g	19%
Sugars 5g	0%
Protein 26g	0%
*Percent daily values are based on a 2,000-calorie diet	

shrimp gumbo

Gumbo is a hearty, thick soup, almost a stew. This New Orleans classic should be served with a scoop of boiled rice.

❖

1 tsp paprika
1 Tsp dried thyme
1 Tbsp all-purpose flour
12-oz monkfish fillet, cut into cubes
1 medium onion, peeled and finely chopped
1 green bell pepper, deseeded, and finely chopped
3 celery stalks, trimmed and finely chopped
2 garlic cloves, peeled and finely chopped
6 oz ladies fingers, trimmed and sliced
3 cups fresh fish or vegetable broth
one 14-oz can chopped tomatoes
salt and black pepper
1 bouquet garni
6 oz large shrimp, peeled
juice of 1 lemon
dash of tabasco sauce
1 Tbsp Worcestershire sauce
3 cups freshly boiled white rice

❖

PREPARATION TIME / 10 MINUTES
COOKING TIME / 55 MINUTES
serves 4

Presoak the claypot as directed. Sprinkle the paprika, thyme, and flour onto a plate. Toss the monkfish cubes in the mixture and place in the claypot. Stir in the onion, garlic, celery, green bell pepper, and ladies fingers. Pour over the broth and tomatoes. Season well and add the bouquet garni.

Cover and place in a cold oven. Set the oven to 425°, and cook for 40 minutes.

Stir in the remaining ingredients except the rice, cover, and cook for a further 15 minutes. Discard the bouquet garni and serve in bowls, ladled over the hot rice.

PICTURED RIGHT.

NUTRITION FACTS

Serving size 1 (696g)

Calories 347   Calories from fat 27

	% daily value*
Total fat 3g	4%
Saturated fat 1g	3%
Cholesterol 86mg	29%
Sodium 410mg	17%
Total carbohydrate 53g	18%
Dietary fiber 3g	13%
Sugars 6g	0%
Protein 26g	0%

*Percent daily values are based on a 2,000-calorie diet

curried lentil and turkey soup

The mild curry flavor in this dish enhances the lentils and turkey. This is a tasty way to use up leftover turkey meat, and it makes a simple supper dish when served with warm bread.

❖

1 large onion, peeled and chopped
2 garlic cloves, peeled and finely chopped
2 carrots, peeled and finely diced
2 stalks celery, trimmed and diced
1 cup red lentils, rinsed in cold water
2 tsp ground coriander
1 tsp ground cumin
6 cardamom pods, split
1 bay leaf
1½ quarts fresh vegetable broth, cooled
salt and black pepper
1 cup cooked turkey meat, shredded
4 Tbsp plain yogurt
one 1-inch piece cucumber, coarsely grated
1 shallot, finely shredded
2 tbsp chopped cilantro

❖

PREPARATION TIME / 10 MINUTES
COOKING TIME / 1 HOUR 45 MINUTES
serves 4

Presoak the claypot as directed. Place the onion, garlic, carrots, and celery in the pot, and stir in the lentils, spices, and bay leaf. Pour in the broth and season well. Cover and place in a cold oven. Set the oven to 400° and cook for 1½ hours.

Stir in the turkey, cover, and cook for a further 15 minutes until the lentils are soft. Discard the bay leaf and cardamom pods, and check the seasoning.

Ladle into warmed soup bowls and serve each portion topped with a spoonful of yogurt, sprinkled with cucumber, shallot, and cilantro. Accompany with warm bread if liked.

NUTRITION FACTS

Serving size 1 (580g)

Calories 329   Calories from fat 45

	% daily value*
Total fat 5g	8%
Saturated fat 1g	5%
Cholesterol 30mg	10%
Sodium 1724mg	72%
Total carbohydrate 45g	15%
Dietary fiber 19g	77%
Sugars 9g	0%
Protein 30g	0%

*Percent daily values are based on a 2,000-calorie diet

beetroot soup

Based on the Russian classic, Borscht, this vegetable soup is both brightly colored and flavorful. The strong red color of the beetroot will discolor your claypot, so some careful soaking will be necessary.

❧

1 lb raw beetroot, peeled and coarsely grated

1 tbsp white wine vinegar

1 quart fresh vegetable broth, cooled

2 medium red onions, peeled and chopped

2 carrots, peeled and coarsely grated

1 large potato, peeled and diced

2 garlic cloves, peeled and minced

1 small white cabbage, finely shredded

2 tsp light brown sugar

1 tsp ground allspice

salt and black pepper

4 Tbsp plain yogurt

4 tsp caraway seeds

2 Tbsp chopped parsley

❧

PREPARATION TIME / 10 MINUTES

COOKING TIME / 2 HOURS 5 MINUTES

serves 4

Presoak the claypot as directed. Place the beetroot in the pot and sprinkle with the vinegar. Pour over half the broth and place in a cold oven. Set the oven to 400° and cook for 1½ hours.

Heat the remaining broth until hot, but not boiling. Stir in the remaining ingredients (except the yogurt, caraway seeds, and parsley) and the hot broth. Cover and bake for a further 30–35 minutes until tender. To serve, ladle into warmed soup bowls and spoon over a tablespoon of yogurt onto each portion. Sprinkle with caraway seeds and chopped parsley to serve.

PICTURED LEFT.

NUTRITION FACTS	
Serving size 1 (486g)	
Calories 167 Calories from fat 9	
	% daily value*
Total fat 1g	1%
Saturated fat 0g	0%
Cholesterol 0mg	0%
Sodium 305mg	13%
Total carbohydrate 36g	12%
Dietary fiber 3g	13%
Sugars 6g	0%
Protein 5g	0%
*Percent daily values are based on a 2,000-calorie diet	

chicken and corn chowder

Traditionally laced with heavy cream, this lighter version is just as flavorful. The addition of parsley dumplings makes it a satisfying and delicious dish.

❧

four 8-oz chicken quarters

2 large onions, shredded

4 bay leaves

salt and black pepper

3 cups fresh chicken broth

1 cup self-rising flour

½ cup vegetable suet

3 Tbsp chopped parsley

1½ cups skim milk

1 cup sweetcorn kernels, defrosted if frozen

❧

PREPARATION TIME / 10 MINUTES

COOKING TIME / 1 HOUR 20 MINUTES

serves 4

Presoak the claypot as directed. Trim away all the excess fat and skin from the chicken. Wash well under cold running water and dry using paper towels.

Place the chopped onions in the base of the claypot and push the bay leaves into the onion. Place the chicken quarters, skinned-side down, on top. Season well. Pour over the broth, cover the pot, and place in a cold oven. Set the oven to 425° and cook for 1 hour until the chicken is done.

Just before the end of cooking, sift the flour into a bowl and stir in the suet, parsley, and some seasoning. Bind together with sufficient cold water to form a soft but not sticky dough. Divide into 16 small rounds. Set aside.

Drain the chicken and, working quickly, strip away all the flesh from the bones, then slice into strips. While working on the chicken, keep the claypot wrapped in clean dish towels to prevent it cooling down. Blot the surface of the soup with paper towels then stir in the cooked chicken, milk, and sweetcorn. Discard the bay leaves. Drop the dumplings onto the surface of the soup. Continue to cook, uncovered, for a further 20 minutes. Check the seasoning to serve.

NUTRITION FACTS	
Serving size 1 (613g)	
Calories 534 Calories from fat 72	
	% daily value*
Total fat 8g	13%
Saturated fat 2g	11%
Cholesterol 150mg	50%
Sodium 3626mg	151%
Total carbohydrate 45g	15%
Dietary fiber 4g	16%
Sugars 7g	0%
Protein 67g	0%
*Percent daily values are based on a 2,000-calorie diet	

black bean and vegetable soup

Black beans are popular in South and Central American cuisine. They have a strong flavor, rather like mushrooms, and are ideal for making soups and stews. If preferred, substitute pinto or borlotti beans.

❖

1¼ cups black beans, soaked overnight

8 oz shallots, peeled and halved

1 large carrot, peeled and finely shredded

2 sticks celery, trimmed and finely shredded

one 14-oz can chopped tomatoes

1 quart fresh vegetable broth, cooled

1 tsp dried sage

salt and black pepper

1 large zucchini, trimmed and diced

4 oz button mushrooms, quartered

fresh sage leaves, to garnish

❖

PREPARATION TIME / 10 MINUTES
PLUS OVERNIGHT SOAKING
COOKING TIME / 2 HOURS 40 MINUTES
serves 4

Drain and rinse the beans. Place in a saucepan, and cover with cold water. Bring to a boil and boil rapidly for 10 minutes. Drain well and cool for 10 minutes.

Presoak the claypot as directed. Place the shallots, carrot, and celery in the pot and stir in the black beans, chopped tomatoes, and broth. Sprinkle over the sage and season well. Cover and place in a cold oven. Set the oven to 400° and cook for 2 hours, stirring occasionally.

Stir in the zucchini and mushrooms. Cover and cook for a further 30 minutes until tender and thick. Check the seasoning and serve garnished with sage leaves.

For an alternative, nonvegetarian version of this soup, omit the mushrooms and stir in a cup cooked, shredded chicken, turkey or ham along with the zucchini.

PICTURED RIGHT.

NUTRITION FACTS	
Serving size 1 (587g)	
Calories 332	Calories from fat 9
	% daily value*
Total fat 1g	2%
Saturated fat 0g	2%
Cholesterol 0mg	0%
Sodium 281mg	12%
Total carbohydrate 66g	22%
Dietary fiber 12g	49%
Sugars 8g	0%
Protein 18g	0%

*Percent daily values are based on a 2,000-calorie diet

potato, apple, and peanut soup

An unusual but surprisingly delicious combination. Peanuts have a high fat content but, used sparingly, their strong flavor adds interest to a vegetable soup.

❖

1 lb potatoes, peeled and finely diced

1 lb apples, peeled, cored and diced

1 Tbsp lemon juice

1 large leek, trimmed and finely shredded

1 Tbsp chopped fresh thyme or 1 tsp dried

1 quart fresh vegetable broth, cooled

salt and black pepper

2 Tbsp smooth peanut butter

1½ cups skim milk

2 Tbsp roasted peanuts, minced

fresh thyme, to garnish

❖

PREPARATION TIME / 10 MINUTES
COOKING TIME / 1 HOUR 30 MINUTES
serves 4

Presoak the claypot as directed. Place the potatoes and apple in the pot and toss in the lemon juice. Stir in the leeks, thyme, broth, and seasoning. Cover and place in a cold oven. Set the oven to 425° and cook for 1 hour 15 minutes.

Place the peanut butter in a small saucepan and gradually blend in the milk. Heat until hot but not boiling and then pour into the pot, cover, and cook for a further 15 minutes. Transfer the soup to a blender and process for a few seconds until smooth.

Serve ladled into warmed soup bowls and sprinkle with minced peanuts. Garnish and accompany with some good bread.

NUTRITION FACTS	
Serving size 1 (623g)	
Calories 329	Calories from fat 63
	% daily value*
Total fat 7g	11%
Saturated fat 1g	7%
Cholesterol 2mg	1%
Sodium 350mg	15%
Total carbohydrate 61g	20%
Dietary fiber 6g	22%
Sugars 22g	0%
Protein 10g	0%

*Percent daily values are based on a 2,000-calorie diet

roast squash and vegetable soup

Dry-roasting a selection of vegetables in a claypot with herbs makes them sweeter and enhances their flavor. No added oil is necessary and because they cook in their own juices these vegetables make an excellent base for a soup.

1 small butternut squash, cut into quarters and deseeded
1 red bell pepper, halved and deseeded
1 yellow bell pepper, halved and deseeded
2 red onions, peeled and cut into quarters
2 large tomatoes, halved
2 garlic cloves, peeled and minced
sprigs of fresh rosemary or 2 tsp dried
1 quart fresh vegetable broth
salt and black pepper
sprigs of rosemary, to garnish

PREPARATION TIME / 10 MINUTES
COOKING TIME / 1 HOUR 5 MINUTES
serves 4

Presoak the claypot as directed. Arrange the squash, bell peppers, and onion in the base of the pot. Arrange the tomatoes on top, and sprinkle over the minced garlic and the rosemary. Cover and place in a cold oven. Set the oven to 425°. Cook for 1 hour until the vegetables have softened.

Carefully remove the vegetables from the pot. Scoop out the flesh from the squash and place in a blender with the onion, garlic, tomatoes, and 3 cups broth. Blend until smooth. Alternatively, mash the vegetables with a fork and then push through a strainer.

Shred the bell peppers. Place in a large saucepan along with the puréed vegetables and remaining broth. Heat through for 4–5 minutes until hot. Check the seasoning and serve ladled into warmed soup bowls. Garnish with rosemary and serve with toasted bread.

PICTURED LEFT.

NUTRITION FACTS	
Serving size 1 (465g)	
Calories 102	Calories from fat 9
	% daily value*
Total fat 1g	1%
Saturated fat 0g	0%
Cholesterol 0mg	0%
Sodium 244mg	10%
Total carbohydrate 23g	8%
Dietary fiber 2g	7%
Sugars 5g	0%
Protein 3g	0%
*Percent daily values are based on a 2,000-calorie diet	

manhattan clam chowder

This recipe uses a combination of canned and fresh clams. For the best results use small fresh clams because they have a sweeter flavor. However, if preferred, you can double the amount of canned clams and omit the fresh.

4 slices bacon, trimmed and finely chopped
1 large onion, peeled and finely diced
2 medium carrots, peeled and finely diced
1 large potato, peeled and finely diced
two 14-oz cans chopped tomatoes
1 cup dry white wine
1 tsp dried thyme
ground cayenne pepper
salt and black pepper
one 20-oz can baby clams, drained and rinsed
1 lb fresh baby clams, scrubbed
2 Tbsp chopped parsley, to garnish
2 slices broiled bacon, chopped, to garnish

PREPARATION TIME / 10 MINUTES
COOKING TIME / 1 HOUR 30 MINUTES
serves 4

Presoak the claypot as directed. Place the raw bacon, onion, carrots, and potato in the pot and mix well. Pour over the tomatoes and wine. Sprinkle with thyme, cayenne, and seasoning.

Cover and place in a cold oven. Set the oven to 425° and cook for 1 hour 15 minutes, stirring occasionally. Stir in both the canned and fresh clams. Cover and cook for a further 15 minutes until the clams have opened.

Discard any clams which have not opened. Check the seasoning and serve sprinkled with chopped parsley and cooked bacon.

NUTRITION FACTS	
Serving size 1 (527g)	
Calories 439	Calories from fat 126
	% daily value*
Total fat 14g	21%
Saturated fat 6g	28%
Cholesterol 59mg	20%
Sodium 13740mg	572%
Total carbohydrate 53g	18%
Dietary fiber 4g	17%
Sugars 9g	0%
Protein 18g	0%
*Percent daily values are based on a 2,000-calorie diet	

creole chicken soup

This thick, spicy soup is an ideal way to use up leftover roast chicken. If you have a leftover carcass, make your own chicken broth for this recipe by boiling it in plenty of water with a few herbs and vegetables.

◇

1 large onion, peeled and chopped
3 stalks celery, trimmed, leaves reserved, and sticks sliced
8 oz ladies fingers, trimmed and thickly sliced
1 large green bell pepper, deseeded and shredded
⅔ cup long-grain rice, rinsed in cold water
one 14-oz can chopped tomatoes
2 bay leaves
1 quart fresh chicken or vegetable broth, cooled
1 Tbsp chopped fresh thyme or 1 tsp dried
salt and black pepper
½–1 tsp hot pepper sauce
1 cup cooked, diced chicken meat
1 cup dry white wine

◇

PREPARATION TIME / 10 MINUTES
COOKING TIME / 1 HOUR 30 MINUTES
serves 4

Presoak the claypot as directed. Place the onion, celery, ladies fingers, green bell pepper, and rice in the claypot and mix well.

Mix the tomatoes, bay leaves, and broth and pour over the rice and vegetables. Sprinkle with thyme and seasoning. Cover the pot and place in a cold oven. Set the oven at 425°. Cook for 1 hour 15 minutes.

Stir in the pepper sauce to taste and add the chicken and wine. Mix well, cover, and continue to cook for a further 15 minutes. Discard the bay leaves, check the seasoning if necessary, and serve sprinkled with the reserved celery leaves.

PICTURED RIGHT.

NUTRITION FACTS	
Serving size 1 (658g)	
Calories 285	Calories from fat 36
	% daily value*
Total fat 4g	7%
Saturated fat 1g	6%
Cholesterol 48mg	16%
Sodium 3643mg	152%
Total carbohydrate 26g	9%
Dietary fiber 4g	18%
Sugars 6g	0%
Protein 27g	0%
*Percent daily values are based on a 2,000-calorie diet	

rich onion and cheese soup

This delicious combination of sweet onions and shallots cooked in a rich beef and red wine broth makes an excellent appetizer, or a light meal when served with crusty bread.

◇

2 large red onions, peeled and finely chopped
1 cup shallots, peeled and finely shredded
2 Tbsp lemon juice
2 garlic cloves, peeled and finely chopped
1 tsp dried thyme
3 cups fresh beef broth
1 cup dry red wine
salt and black pepper
2 tsp superfine sugar
½ cup low-fat Cheddar cheese, grated
2 Tbsp chopped parsley

◇

PREPARATION TIME / 10 MINUTES
COOKING TIME / APPROXIMATELY 1 HOUR 30 MINUTES
serves 4

Presoak the claypot as directed. Place the onions and shallots in the pot, and mix in the lemon juice to coat well. Stir in the garlic and thyme.

Pour in the broth and red wine, and season well. Cover and place in a cold oven. Set the oven to 425° and cook for about 1 hour 15 minutes, stirring occasionally, until the onions are tender.

Stir in the sugar and adjust the seasoning if necessary. Stir in the cheese, cover again, and cook for a further 5 minutes until melted. Stir well to distribute the cheese. Serve immediately, sprinkled with chopped parsley.

NUTRITION FACTS	
Serving size 1 (313g)	
Calories 201	Calories from fat 36
	% daily value*
Total fat 4g	7%
Saturated fat 3g	17%
Cholesterol 12mg	4%
Sodium 838mg	35%
Total carbohydrate 18g	6%
Dietary fiber 1g	4%
Sugars 2g	0%
Protein 13g	0%
*Percent daily values are based on a 2,000-calorie diet	

fish and seafood

sole and salmon roulades with lemon and watercress sauce

Sole is a very delicately flavored white fish. Rolled with a filling of smoked salmon and herbs and served with an accompaniment of green vegetables, it makes an elegant and impressive dish which is ideal for entertaining.

four 4-oz sole fillets
4 oz smoked salmon
¼ cup low-fat soft cheese flavored with garlic and herbs
1 Tbsp chopped dill
1 lemon
salt and black pepper
dill and lemon rind, to garnish

for the sauce

¾ cup plain yogurt
sprigs of fresh watercress, trimmed
2 Tbsp lemon juice
1 tsp finely grated lemon rind

PREPARATION TIME / 10 MINUTES
COOKING TIME / 40 MINUTES
serves 4

Soak the claypot as directed and line the base with waxed paper. Skin the sole fillets by inserting a small sharp knife between the skin and flesh at the tail end. Holding the skin taut, strip the flesh away in one piece. Halve the fillets lengthways. Place strips of smoked salmon over the skinned side of each fillet, trimming if necessary.

Beat the soft cheese to soften and spread a little over the smoked salmon. Sprinkle with a little chopped dill, and carefully roll up from the head to the tail end. Place the fish rolls, seam-side down, in the pot. Slice the lemon into 8 wedges and squeeze 2 over the rolls. Arrange the others around the fish. Season.

Place in a cold oven and set the oven to 425°. Cover and cook for 35–40 minutes until the fish is done. Just before the end of the cooking time, place all the sauce ingredients in a small saucepan and heat through gently without boiling until hot.

NUTRITION FACTS	
Serving size 1 (156g)	
Calories 128	Calories from fat 36
	% daily value*
Total fat 4g	7%
Saturated fat 2g	11%
Cholesterol 30mg	10%
Sodium 501mg	21%
Total carbohydrate 9g	3%
Dietary fiber 0g	2%
Sugars 4g	0%
Protein 15g	0%
*Percent daily values are based on a 2,000-calorie diet	

cod with mushrooms

Mushrooms complement fish extremely well. In this recipe you can use any variety you like, although the meatier ones like shiitake work particularly well.

◇

1½ lb piece cod fillet, skinned
1 bunch scallions, trimmed and shredded
6 oz assorted mushrooms such as shiitake, button, chanterelle, or morel, sliced or quartered
½ cup peeled shrimp, defrosted if frozen
4 Tbsp oyster sauce
2 Tbsp dry sherry
salt and black pepper
1–2 tsp cornstarch mixed with 1 Tbsp cold water
chives, to garnish

◇

PREPARATION TIME / 5 MINUTES
COOKING TIME / 40 MINUTES
serves 4

Soak the claypot as directed, and line the base with waxed paper. Wash the cod fillet and pat dry with paper towels.

Place the cod in the claypot. Sprinkle with the scallions, mushrooms, and shrimp. Mix the oyster sauce and sherry and spoon over the top. Season with salt and black pepper. Cover and place in a cold oven. Set the oven to 425° and cook for 35–40 minutes until done.

Carefully remove the fish and vegetables from the claypot using a pancake turner and place on a warmed serving plate. Strain off the juices into a saucepan and add the cornstarch paste. Heat, stirring, until thickened.

Using a pair of scissors, snip the chives over the fish and serve immediately, with the thickened cooking juices poured over it.

PICTURED RIGHT.

NUTRITION FACTS

Serving size 1 (164g)

Calories 155	Calories from fat 9

	% daily value*
Total fat 1g	2%
Saturated fat 0g	1%
Cholesterol 74mg	25%
Sodium 562mg	23%
Total carbohydrate 14g	5%
Dietary fiber 1g	3%
Sugars 1g	0%
Protein 20g	0%

*Percent daily values are based on a 2,000-calorie diet

cajun fish

Traditionally, this dish of fish, invented in New Orleans, involved dipping the fish in a rich blend of butter and spices and sealing it in a very hot pan to "blacken" it. This version uses the same spices, but the fish is cooked in the oven, keeping it tender and moist.

◇

four 6-oz white fish fillets, such as cod, sea bass or halibut, about ½ inch thick
wedges of lime, and chopped thyme, to garnish

for the spice mix

1 Tbsp paprika
1 shallot, peeled and chopped very fine
1 garlic clove, peeled and minced
½ tsp salt
½ tsp ground cumin
½ tsp cayenne pepper
½ tsp ground black pepper
1 tsp dried thyme

◇

PREPARATION TIME / 5 MINUTES
COOKING TIME / 40 MINUTES
serves 4

Presoak the claypot as directed and line the base with waxed paper. Wash the fish fillets, pat dry and set aside.

Mix together all the ingredients for the spice mix to form a paste, then spread a thin layer over both sides of the fish fillets, making sure they are completely coated.

Arrange the spiced fish in the claypot. Cover and place in a cold oven. Set the oven to 425° and cook for 30–40 minutes until the fish is done. Serve garnished with lime wedges and chopped thyme with a crisp salad and some boiled rice.

NUTRITION FACTS

Serving size 1 (195g)

Calories 157	Calories from fat 18

	% daily value*
Total fat 2g	2%
Saturated fat 0g	1%
Cholesterol 73mg	24%
Sodium 385mg	16%
Total carbohydrate 4g	1%
Dietary fiber 1g	5%
Sugars 0g	0%
Protein 31g	0%

*Percent daily values are based on a 2,000-calorie diet

sea bass on a bed of oriental vegetables

When mature, a whole sea bass extends to nearly a yard in length. It is a fine-flaked white fish, free of small bones. Firm steaks work best in this recipe because they hold their shape well during baking.

2 large carrots, peeled and cut into julienne strips
1 red bell pepper, deseeded and finely sliced
1 yellow bell pepper, deseeded and finely sliced
4 oz snow peas, trimmed and finely shredded
1 large zucchini, trimmed and cut into julienne strips
1 large leek, trimmed and shredded
one 1-inch piece ginger root, peeled and finely shredded
2 garlic cloves, peeled and minced
four 6-oz sea bass steaks
2 tsp Chinese five-spice powder
2 tbsp dark soy sauce
2 Tbsp rice wine or sweet sherry
shredded leek and chives, to garnish

PREPARATION TIME / 10 MINUTES
COOKING TIME / 40 MINUTES
serves 4

Presoak the claypot as directed. Place all the vegetables inside, together with the ginger and cloves, and mix well.

Wash and pat dry the sea bass steaks using paper towels. Rub the flesh side with the five-spice powder and arrange the steaks on the top of the vegetables. Mix the soy sauce and rice wine or sherry together and spoon over the fish and vegetables.

Cover and place in a cold oven. Set the oven to 425° and cook for 35–40 minutes until the fish is done. Serve each fish steak on a bed of the vegetables, garnish, and serve with boiled noodles.

PICTURED LEFT.

NUTRITION FACTS	
Serving size 1 (460g)	
Calories 273 Calories from fat 36	
	% daily value*
Total fat 4g	6%
Saturated fat 1g	5%
Cholesterol 70mg	24%
Sodium 712mg	30%
Total carbohydrate 22g	7%
Dietary fiber 4g	17%
Sugars 7g	0%
Protein 36g	0%
*Percent daily values are based on a 2,000-calorie diet	

mediterranean fish stew

This is a favorite combination of fish and shellfish found throughout the shores and ports of the Mediterranean. Gentle stewing is an excellent way to maintain their flavor and moist texture.

1 large onion, peeled and chopped
2 garlic cloves, peeled and minced
4 baby eggplants, sliced
1 large zucchini, trimmed and diced
1 orange bell pepper, deseeded and chopped
two 14-oz cans chopped tomatoes
1 cup fresh fish broth
1 cup dry red wine
2 tsp superfine sugar
1 bouquet garni
salt and black pepper
1 lb thick cod fillet, skinned and cubed
1½ lb fresh mussels, scrubbed
8 oz baby squid, cleaned, trimmed, and cut into rings
8 oz large raw shrimp

PREPARATION TIME / 15 MINUTES
COOKING TIME / 1 HOUR 30 MINUTES
serves 4

Presoak the claypot as directed. Place the onion, garlic, eggplants, zucchini, and bell pepper in the pot and mix well. Stir in the tomatoes, broth, wine, and sugar. Add the bouquet garni and season well. Cover and place in a cold oven. Set the oven to 425° and cook for 1 hour.

Stir in the cod, mussels, squid, and shrimp. Cover and cook for a further 30 minutes until the fish is tender, the mussels have opened, and the shrimp are pink.

Discard any mussels that have failed to open, and remove the bouquet garni. Serve straight from the pot with plenty of French bread to mop up the sauce.

NUTRITION FACTS	
Serving size 1 (975g)	
Calories 496 Calories from fat 63	
	% daily value*
Total fat 7g	11%
Saturated fat 1g	7%
Cholesterol 315mg	105%
Sodium 1039mg	43%
Total carbohydrate 34g	11%
Dietary fiber 6g	26%
Sugars 14g	0%
Protein 64g	0%
*Percent daily values are based on a 2,000-calorie diet	

cuban-style fish and rice

This recipe is similar to the Spanish Paella but with the addition of sweet spices and dark rum. It is a very hearty dish and requires only a crisp salad or some bread as an accompaniment.

❖

1 lb skinless firm white fish fillets, such as monkfish, halibut or cod, cut into
1-inch cubes
1 tsp ground cumin
1 tsp dried oregano
1 tsp ground cinnamon
juice of 1 lime
salt and black pepper
1 large onion, peeled and chopped
2 garlic cloves, peeled and minced
1 red, 1 yellow, and 1 green bell pepper, deseeded and chopped
1¼ cups long-grain rice, rinsed
5 cups fresh vegetable broth
large pinch of saffron
¾ cup dark rum

❖

PREPARATION TIME / 15 MINUTES PLUS STANDING
COOKING TIME / 1 HOUR 45 MINUTES
serves 4

Presoak the claypot as directed. In a shallow bowl, mix together the fish, cumin, oregano, cinnamon, lime juice, and seasoning. Cover and chill until required.

Place the onion, garlic, bell peppers, and rice into the claypot and mix well. Pour over the broth and sprinkle in the saffron. Season well. Cover and place in a cold oven. Set the oven to 425° and cook for 1 hour 15 minutes, stirring occasionally. Stir in the marinated fish and rum, mix well, cover, and cook for a further 30 minutes until the fish is tender and the rice has absorbed most of the liquid. Stand, covered, for 10 minutes to absorb any remaining liquid. Check the seasoning and serve straight from the claypot.

PICTURED RIGHT.

NUTRITION FACTS	
Serving size 1 (671g)	
Calories 347	Calories from fat 9
	% daily value*
Total fat 1g	2%
Saturated fat 0g	1%
Cholesterol 42mg	14%
Sodium 335mg	14%
Total carbohydrate 35g	12%
Dietary fiber 3g	12%
Sugars 3g	0%
Protein 25g	0%

*Percent daily values are based on a 2,000-calorie diet

swordfish with citrus and chili butter

Only a very small amount of butter is needed in the recipe, and it is packed full with the flavor of lemon, chile, and cilantro. Serve the steaks simply with a crisp salad and some bread.

❖

four 6-oz swordfish steaks
1 Tbsp lemon juice
1 tsp ground coriander
lemon wedges, sliced red chile, and cilantro to garnish

for the butter

2 Tbsp butter, softened
½ tsp finely grated lemon rind
1 tsp lemon juice
1 small red chile, deseeded and finely chopped
1 Tbsp chopped cilantro
black pepper

❖

PREPARATION TIME / 10 MINUTES PLUS CHILLING
COOKING TIME / 40 MINUTES
serves 4

Presoak the claypot as directed, and line with waxed paper. Wash and pat dry the swordfish steaks using paper towels. Using a small sharp knife, score one side of the flesh in a crisscross pattern. Place the steaks in the claypot and sprinkle with the lemon juice and ground coriander.

For the butter, mix all the ingredients together until well blended and then pile on to a piece of waxed paper. Roll up and place in the freezer for 10 minutes until firm. Unwrap and slice, and place a piece of the butter on top of each fish steak.

Cover and place in a cold oven. Set the oven to 425° and cook for 35–40 minutes until the fish is tender and done.

Drain the fish and serve, garnished, and accompanied by a crisp salad and some warm bread.

NUTRITION FACTS	
Serving size 1 (192g)	
Calories 267	Calories from fat 117
	% daily value*
Total fat 13g	20%
Saturated fat 6g	28%
Cholesterol 83mg	28%
Sodium 216mg	9%
Total carbohydrate 2g	1%
Dietary fiber 0g	2%
Sugars 0g	0%
Protein 34g	0%

*Percent daily values are based on a 2,000-calorie diet

trout stuffed with tabbouleh

Whole trout bake very successfully in the claypot. This dish of tender fish, bulgur wheat, diced salad vegetables, and the fresh flavors of mint and parsley, is perfect for a light summer lunch or supper.

❧

four 8-oz trout, cleaned and heads removed
salt and black pepper
4 Tbsp dry white wine
lemon wedges, mint, and parsley, to garnish

for the stuffing

½ cup bulgur wheat, soaked according to the manufacturer's instructions
¼ cup finely diced cucumber
4 medium tomatoes, seeded and finely chopped
4 scallions, trimmed and finely chopped
2 Tbsp chopped mint
2 Tbsp chopped parsley
1 Tbsp lemon juice
¾ cup plain yogurt
2 Tbsp chopped mint
2 Tbsp chopped parsley

❧

PREPARATION TIME / 10 MINUTES
COOKING TIME / 45 MINUTES
serves 4

Presoak the claypot as directed and line the bottom with waxed paper. Wash the trout inside and out, and pat dry using paper towels. Season the cavities with salt and pepper, and set aside.

For the stuffing, mix all the ingredients together, except the yogurt, and reserving some mint and parsley for garnish, to serve, and season. Spoon some stuffing into the cavity of each trout and transfer them to the claypot. Any remaining stuffing mixture can be chilled and served as a salad accompaniment. Spoon the white wine over the trout, cover, and place in a cold oven. Set the oven to 425° and cook for 45 minutes or until the trout are done.

Just before the end of cooking, blend the yogurt, mint, parsley, and seasoning together. Carefully remove the trout from the pot, garnish with lemon wedges, mint leaves, and sprigs of parsley, and serve with the sauce. PICTURED LEFT.

NUTRITION FACTS	
Serving size 1 (508g)	
Calories 434 Calories from fat 81	
	% daily value*
Total fat 9g	14%
Saturated fat 2g	12%
Cholesterol 189mg	63%
Sodium 328mg	14%
Total carbohydrate 38g	13%
Dietary fiber 7g	28%
Sugars 8g	0%
Protein 46g	0%
*Percent daily values are based on a 2,000-calorie diet	

mussel and clam bake

Shellfish is easy to cook in the claypot, with very successful results. These popular mollusks are cooked simply with white wine, herbs, and garlic. They make a delicious light lunch or an interesting appetizer.

❧

1½ lb fresh baby clams
1½ lb fresh mussels
1 medium red onion, peeled and very finely chopped
1 garlic clove, peeled and minced
1 Tbsp lemon juice
4 bay leaves
¼ tsp dried red chili flakes (optional)
1 cup dry white wine
salt and black pepper
4 Tbsp heavy cream
4 Tbsp chopped parsley

❧

PREPARATION TIME / 10 MINUTES
COOKING TIME / 40 MINUTES
serves 4

Presoak the claypot as directed. Using a stiff brush, scrub the clams and mussels under cold running water to remove any sand; remove the feathery beards which protrude from the mussels.

Pile the clams and mussels into the claypot. Carefully mix in the onion and garlic, and sprinkle with lemon juice. Push the bay leaves in between the shells and sprinkle over the dried chili if using. Pour in the wine and season well. Cover and place in a cold oven. Set the oven to 425° and cook for 20 minutes. Holding the pot and lid very firmly, carefully give the mussels and clams a good shake, then cook for a further 15 minutes, until they have opened. Discard the bay leaves.

Using a slotted spoon, transfer the mussels and clams into four warmed serving bowls. Discard any that have failed to open. Gently mix the cream and parsley into the cooking juices and then ladle over the shellfish. Serve immediately, with some good bread to mop up the juices.

NUTRITION FACTS	
Serving size 1 (428g)	
Calories 458 Calories from fat 63	
	% daily value*
Total fat 7g	11%
Saturated fat 1g	5%
Cholesterol 162mg	54%
Sodium 848mg	35%
Total carbohydrate 20g	7%
Dietary fiber 1g	4%
Sugars 1g	0%
Protein 64g	0%
*Percent daily values are based on a 2,000-calorie diet	

swordfish with tomatoes and orange

A firm, lightly oily fish, swordfish is perfect for claypot cooking, although care should be taken not to overcook it or it can become "woolly" in texture. Here it stays succulent on a bed of seasoned tomatoes.

◧

2 lb ripe tomatoes, quartered
1 bulb fennel, trimmed, fronds reserved, and sliced
1 large red onion, peeled and shredded
2 tsp superfine sugar
salt and black pepper
four 6-oz swordfish steaks
4 scallions, trimmed and finely chopped
sprigs of tarragon, chervil, and marjoram
2 oranges

◧

PREPARATION TIME / 10 MINUTES
COOKING TIME / 40 MINUTES
serves 4

Presoak the claypot as directed. Place the tomatoes, fennel, and red onion in the pot and mix well. Sprinkle with the sugar and seasoning.

Wash and pat dry the swordfish steaks. Season and place on top of the tomato mixture. Sprinkle with the scallions. Roughly chop the herbs and sprinkle over the fish. Grate the rind of the oranges over the fish. Cover and place in a cold oven. Set the oven to 425° and bake for 35–40 minutes until the swordfish is done.

Meanwhile, slice off the tops and bottoms of the oranges, and then remove the skin and as much white pith as possible. Cut in between the membranes and pull out the segments. Set aside.

Serve the fish with the tomato mixture and a few orange segments. Garnish with the fennel fronds.

PICTURED RIGHT.

NUTRITION FACTS	
Serving size 1 (508g)	
Calories 309	Calories from fat 72
	% daily value*
Total fat 8g	12%
Saturated fat 2g	10%
Cholesterol 66mg	22%
Sodium 332mg	14%
Total carbohydrate 24g	8%
Dietary fiber 5g	20%
Sugars 15g	0%
Protein 37g	0%

*Percent daily values are based on a 2,000-calorie diet

sesame salmon with cucumber

The fresh, delicate flavor of cucumber makes it the perfect accompaniment to salmon. In this recipe, sesame is also used to add a slight nuttiness, and red chile for an added kick.

◧

1 large cucumber
2 Tbsp salt
1 Tbsp rice wine vinegar
2 tsp superfine sugar
1 red chile, deseeded and finely chopped
four 5-oz salmon steaks
2 tsp sesame oil
salt and black pepper
1 Tbsp toasted sesame seeds
chives, cucumber, and red chile, to garnish

◧

PREPARATION TIME / 10 MINUTES PLUS SALTING
COOKING TIME / 40 MINUTES
serves 4

Presoak the claypot as directed. Using a vegetable peeler, peel off all the skin from the cucumber. Slice in half lengthways and scoop out the seeds. Slice the flesh into diagonal slices ½-inch thick. Place in a bowl and sprinkle with salt. Set aside for 30 minutes.

Rinse the cucumber well to wash off all the salt and dry using paper towels. Transfer to the claypot and sprinkle with vinegar, sugar, and chile. Wash and pat dry the salmon steaks using paper towels and place on top of the cucumber. Brush with the sesame oil and season.

Cover and place in a cold oven. Set the oven to 425° and cook for 35–40 minutes until the salmon is done.

Drain the salmon and cucumber and serve sprinkled with the toasted sesame seeds, garnished with chopped chives and a little chopped chile, and accompanied by boiled new potatoes and steamed vegetables.

NUTRITION FACTS	
Serving size 1 (344g)	
Calories 638	Calories from fat 108
	% daily value*
Total fat 12g	19%
Saturated fat 2g	9%
Cholesterol 78mg	26%
Sodium 3734mg	156%
Total carbohydrate 104g	35%
Dietary fiber 1g	5%
Sugars 100g	0%
Protein 29g	0%

*Percent daily values are based on a 2,000-calorie diet

salmon with a herb crust

A colorful combination of salmon covered in a light fresh herb crust and roasted Mediterranean vegetables makes a stunning course for a celebration meal.

❖

1 large red bell pepper, deseeded and quartered

1 large orange bell pepper, deseeded and quartered

1 large green bell pepper, deseeded and quartered

2 medium red onions, peeled and cut into 6 wedges

2 medium zucchini, trimmed, halved lengthways and thickly sliced

2 garlic cloves, peeled and thinly sliced

4 bay leaves

salt and black pepper

2 Tbsp lemon juice

four 5-oz salmon fillets, skinned

1 Tbsp wholegrain mustard

2 Tbsp sour cream

1 small bunch each of parsley, dill, and tarragon, chopped

2 large beefsteak tomatoes, quartered

❖

PREPARATION TIME / 10 MINUTES

COOKING TIME / 1 HOUR 20 MINUTES

serves 4

Presoak the claypot as directed. Arrange the bell peppers, onion, and courgettes in the pot. Push the sliced garlic and bay leaves into the vegetables. Season well and sprinkle with the lemon juice.

Cover and place in a cold oven. Set the oven to 425° and cook for 40 minutes.

Meanwhile, wash and pat dry the fish fillets using paper towels. Mix the mustard and sour cream and spread over both sides of the salmon. Mix the herbs together and press into the fish to form a thick crust.

Mix the vegetables, push the tomato quarters into them, and arrange the salmon on top. Cover and continue to cook for a further 30 minutes. Remove the lid and cook for 10 minutes longer until done. Drain and serve.

NUTRITION FACTS

Serving size 1 (580g)

Calories 358   Calories from fat 153

	% daily value*
Total fat 17g	26%
Saturated fat 4g	22%
Cholesterol 96mg	32%
Sodium 278mg	12%
Total carbohydrate 20g	7%
Dietary fiber 5g	22%
Sugars 8g	0%
Protein 32g	0%

*Percent daily values are based on a 2,000-calorie diet

tuna with mexican rice

The Mexican flavors of this dish go very well with this firm-textured meaty fish. This makes a filling meal, and needs no more than a light salad to accompany it.

❖

1 large onion, peeled and chopped
2 green chiles, deseeded and finely chopped
2 large green bell peppers, deseeded and diced
1 garlic clove, peeled and minced
1 Tbsp ground coriander
1¼ cups long-grain rice, rinsed in cold water
4 cups fresh vegetable broth
salt and black pepper
⅔ cup frozen peas, thawed
four 6-oz fresh tuna steaks
2 Tbsp lime juice
1 small yellow bell pepper, deseeded and very finely diced
1 small red bell pepper, deseeded and very finely diced
6 Tbsp chopped cilantro
lime wedges and cilantro to garnish

❖

PREPARATION TIME / 10 MINUTES PLUS STANDING
COOKING TIME / 1 HOUR 20 MINUTES
serves 4

Presoak the claypot as directed. Place the onion, chiles, green bell pepper, garlic, ground coriander, and rice in the pot and mix well. Pour over the broth and season well. Cover and place in a cold oven. Set the oven to 425° and cook for 50 minutes, stirring occasionally.

Stir the peas into the mixture and arrange the tuna steaks on top of the rice. Sprinkle with the lime juice and chopped bell peppers. Cover and cook for a further 30 minutes until the tuna is done and the rice has absorbed the cooking liquid. Stand, covered, for 10 minutes.

Remove the tuna from the rice, and stir the chopped cilantro into the rice. Place a portion of rice on each serving plate and place a tuna steak on top. Garnish and serve with a crisp salad.

NUTRITION FACTS	
Serving size 1 (705g)	
Calories 406	Calories from fat 27
	% daily value*
Total fat 3g	4%
Saturated fat 1g	3%
Cholesterol 99mg	33%
Sodium 465mg	19%
Total carbohydrate 36g	12%
Dietary fiber 4g	18%
Sugars 5g	0%
Protein 57g	0%

*Percent daily values are based on a 2,000-calorie diet

baked gray mullet with greens

In this dish, gray mullet is baked on a bed of shredded crisp lettuce and sorrel leaves. If sorrel is unavailable, then use baby spinach leaves instead.

❖

1 romaine lettuce, washed and drained
1 cup sorrel leaves, washed and trimmed
2 shallots, peeled and finely shredded
one 2-lb gray mullet, cleaned and scaled
salt and black pepper
1 tsp grated lemon rind
½ cup dry white vermouth
6 Tbsp low-fat natural yogurt
lemon wedges and watercress to garnish

❖

PREPARATION TIME / 10 MINUTES
COOKING TIME / APPROXIMATELY 40 MINUTES
serves 4

Presoak a claypot as directed. Shake any excess water from the lettuce and sorrel. Shred the lettuce and place in the pot. If the sorrel leaves are large, shred them a little, and add to the pot. Stir in the shallots and mix well.

Wash and pat dry the mullet. Season inside and out, and place half the lemon rind in the fish cavity. Place the mullet on the "greens," pour over the vermouth, and sprinkle with remaining lemon rind.

Cover and place in a cold oven. Set oven to 425° and cook for 40 minutes, or until cooked through.

Drain the fish and greens, reserving the juices, and place on a warmed serving dish. Transfer the juices to a saucepan, and stir in the yogurt. Heat gently, without boiling, and adjust the seasoning. Serve the fish garnished with lemon wedges and watercress.

NUTRITION FACTS	
Serving size 1 (348g)	
Calories 329	Calories from fat 81
	% daily value*
Total fat 9g	14%
Saturated fat 3g	14%
Cholesterol 112mg	37%
Sodium 752mg	31%
Total carbohydrate 8g	3%
Dietary fiber 1g	2%
Sugars 4g	0%
Protein 46g	0%

*Percent daily values are based on a 2,000-calorie diet

scallop and bacon kabobs with curried rice

A delicious combination of fruit-flavored curried rice served with tender scallops wrapped in bacon strips. The rice cooks in the bottom of the claypot whilst the kabobs cook in the steam on top.

◈

1 large onion, peeled and chopped

1 red bell pepper, deseeded and diced

1 Tbsp mild curry powder

6 cardamom pods, split

1 bay leaf

1¼ cups long-grain rice, washed

3½ cups fresh vegetable broth

salt and black pepper

16 prepared scallops

4 slices rindless bacon

2 Tbsp lemon juice

¼ cup golden raisins

¼ cup no-soak dried apricots, sliced into thin strips

4 Tbsp chopped cilantro

2 Tbsp toasted slivered almonds, to garnish

◈

PREPARATION TIME / 10 MINUTES
PLUS STANDING
COOKING TIME / 1 HOUR 20 MINUTES
serves 4

Presoak the claypot as directed. Place the onion, bell pepper, curry powder, cardamom pods, bay leaf, and rice in the claypot and mix well. Pour over the broth, and season well. Cover and place in a cold oven. Set the oven to 425° and cook for 1 hour, stirring occasionally.

Meanwhile, wash and pat dry the scallops using paper towels. Cut each bacon slice lengthways into four thin strips, and wrap a strip around each scallop. Thread onto four skewers, place on a plate, and sprinkle with lemon juice. Cover and chill until required.

Stir the raisins and apricots into the rice, and arrange the skewers on top of the rice. Cover and cook for 20 minutes until the scallops are done. Stand, covered, for 10 minutes.

To serve, place the kabobs on warmed serving plates. Discard the bay leaf and cardamoms from the rice, and stir in three tablespoons cilantro. Divide the rice between the serving plates and place a kabob on top of each. Sprinkle with the remaining cilantro, and a few slivered almonds.

NUTRITION FACTS	
Serving size 1 (466g)	
Calories 325	Calories from fat 54
	% daily value*
Total fat 6g	10%
Saturated fat 1g	7%
Cholesterol 45mg	15%
Sodium 534mg	22%
Total carbohydrate 40g	13%
Dietary fiber 4g	17%
Sugars 10g	0%
Protein 27g	0%

*Percent daily values are based on a 2,000-calorie diet

roast monkfish wrapped in ham

The Italian flavors in this dish combine very well with the firm texture of monkfish and its delicate, sweet taste. Serve the fish in slices accompanied by a medley of chopped tomatoes, olives, and basil.

❧

1½ lb monkfish

salt and black pepper

1 bunch basil leaves, washed

1 sun-dried tomato, soaked

6 canned artichoke hearts, drained and chopped

1 garlic clove, peeled and minced

2 Tbsp freshly grated Parmesan cheese

6 thin slices Parma ham

4 plum tomatoes, skinned, deseeded, and chopped

¼ cup pitted black olives, drained and chopped

❧

PREPARATION TIME / 15 MINUTES

COOKING TIME / 50 MINUTES

serves 6

Presoak the claypot as directed, and line the base with waxed paper. Skin the monkfish. Slice in half by cutting along the sides of the central bone.

Lay the fish between two layers of waxed paper and flatten to ½ inch thick with a rolling pin. Peel away the paper and season both pieces. Reserving a few basil leaves, lay the remaining leaves over the seasoned fish.

Finely chop the sun-dried tomato. Mix together with the chopped artichokes, garlic, and Parmesan cheese. Press onto one half of the fish, and top with the other piece of fish. Wrap the ham around the fish, overlapping, to cover. Transfer to the claypot, cover, and place in a cold oven. Set the oven to 425° and cook for 45–50 minutes until the fish is done.

Just before the end of the cooking time, gently heat the plum tomatoes in a small saucepan. Stir in the olives and season. Shred the remaining basil and stir into the tomatoes just before serving. Slice the monkfish and serve with the tomato mixture.

NUTRITION FACTS	
Serving size 1 (292g)	
Calories 209	Calories from fat 63
	% daily value*
Total fat 7g	10%
Saturated fat 2g	9%
Cholesterol 46mg	15%
Sodium 634mg	26%
Total carbohydrate 13g	4%
Dietary fiber 3g	12%
Sugars 4g	0%
Protein 25g	0%

*Percent daily values are based on a 2,000-calorie diet

poultry

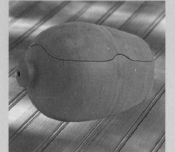

chili chicken, rice 'n peas

"Hoppin' John," "Limpin' Susan," "Moors and Christians" are all names given to the American and West Indian dish of rice and beans. The beans used vary from recipe to recipe, as do the flavorings. This is a mild version with added chicken.

❖

1¼ cups long-grain rice, washed
1 large onion, peeled and finely chopped
1 mild green chile, deseeded and finely chopped
1 small bunch thyme
4 cups fresh chicken broth
salt and pepper
4 Tbsp canned coconut milk
2 large tomatoes, peeled, deseeded, and diced
one 15-oz can beans, such as black-eye, black or kidney, drained and rinsed
1¼ cups cooked chicken
½ cup lean diced ham
sprigs of thyme to garnish

❖

PREPARATION TIME / 10 MINUTES PLUS STANDING
COOKING TIME / 1 HOUR 20 MINUTES
serves 4

Presoak the claypot as directed. Place the rice, onion, and chile in the claypot and push in the bunch of thyme. Pour over the broth and season well. Cover and place in a cold oven. Set the oven to 425° and cook for 30 minutes. Stir the mixture and return to the oven for a further 30 minutes.

Carefully mix in the coconut milk, tomatoes, beans, chicken, and ham. Cover and bake for a further 20 minutes, until the chicken is hot and most of the liquid has been absorbed. Stand, covered, for 10 minutes. Discard the bunch of thyme, and serve straight from the pot garnished with sprigs of thyme.

NUTRITION FACTS	
Serving size 1 (600g)	
Calories 688 Calories from fat 99	
	% daily value*
Total fat 11g	16%
Saturated fat 5g	25%
Cholesterol 82mg	27%
Sodium 1297mg	54%
Total carbohydrate 86g	29%
Dietary fiber 18g	71%
Sugars 2g	0%
Protein 62g	0%

*Percent daily values are based on a 2,000-calorie diet

chicken and vegetable pot roast

In this recipe chicken, potatoes, and vegetables are all cooked together and flavored with herbs and wine.

❖

2 small red bell peppers, deseeded and quartered

2 small yellow bell peppers, deseeded and quartered

1 bulb fennel, trimmed and sliced

2 medium red onions, peeled and quartered

1 lb baby new potatoes, scrubbed

one 3½-lb oven-ready chicken

1 small lemon

salt and black pepper

2 sprigs each of tarragon, marjoram, and rosemary

2 bay leaves

¾ cup dry white wine

fresh herbs and lemon wedges, to garnish

❖

PREPARATION TIME / 15 MINUTES
COOKING TIME / 2 HOURS 15 MINUTES
serves 4

Presoak the claypot as directed. Place the bell peppers, fennel, onions, and potatoes in the pot.

Wash the chicken inside and out and pat dry using paper towels. Halve the lemon and place it inside the chicken. Season all over. Take one sprig of each herb and a bay leaf and tie together with clean string. Repeat with the remaining herbs and bay leaf, forming two bouquet garni. Place one inside the chicken and the other on the vegetables. Place the chicken on the vegetables, spooning the vegetables up around.

Pour in the wine, cover, and place in a cold oven. Set the oven to 425° and cook for 2 hours until the chicken juices run clear. Remove the lid and cook for a further 10 minutes until lightly golden. Discard the bouquet garni and lemon.

Transfer the chicken to a warmed serving platter and surround with the vegetables. Garnish with fresh herbs and lemon wedges to serve.

NUTRITION FACTS	
Serving size 1 (811g)	
Calories 1145 Calories from fat 477	
	% daily value*
Total fat 53g	81%
Saturated fat 15g	74%
Cholesterol 421mg	140%
Sodium 1374mg	57%
Total carbohydrate 44g	15%
Dietary fiber 6g	23%
Sugars 5g	0%
Protein 111g	0%

*Percent daily values are based on a 2,000-calorie diet

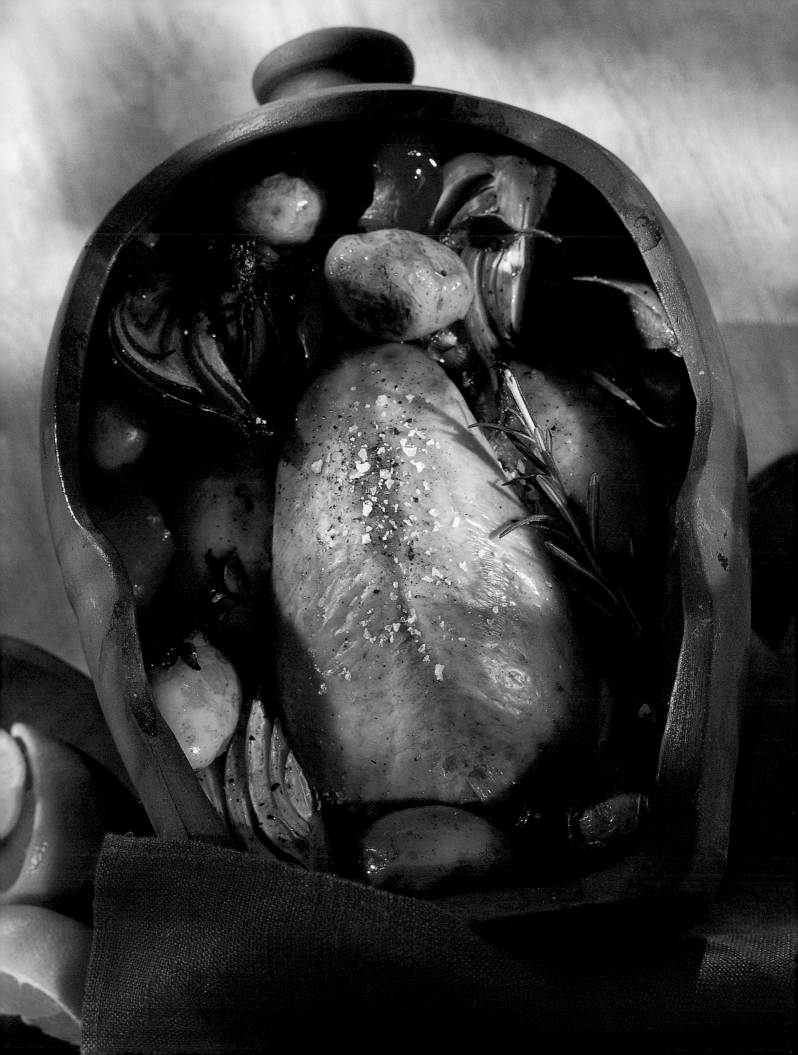

tandoori chicken kabobs

Tandoori baked meats are marinated and dry-roasted in a special clay oven known as a *tandoor*. The marinade contains yogurt which helps to tenderize the meat during cooking. These kabobs are mildly spiced and taste delicious served with a refreshing mango raita.

❖

four 5-oz boneless, skinless chicken breasts, cut into cubes
1 garlic clove, minced
one 1-inch piece ginger root, peeled and finely chopped
1 fresh green chile, deseeded and finely chopped
6 Tbsp plain yogurt
1 Tbsp tomato paste
1 tsp ground cumin
1 tsp ground coriander
1 tsp ground turmeric
salt and black pepper

for the raita

1 small ripe mango, peeled, pitted, and diced
¼ cup finely chopped cucumber
2 Tbsp chopped mint
¾ cup plain yogurt

❖

PREPARATION TIME / 15 MINUTES PLUS MARINADING
COOKING TIME / 40 MINUTES
serves 4

Place the chicken in a shallow dish. Mix together the remaining ingredients for the chicken and spoon over. Mix well, cover, and chill for 2 hours.

Presoak the claypot as directed and line the bottom with waxed paper. Thread the chicken onto eight skewers and arrange in the pot. Brush with any yogurt mixture that is left over. Cover and place in a cold oven. Set the oven to 425° and cook for 30–40 minutes until tender.

Just before the end of cooking, mix together the raita ingredients in a bowl, cover, and chill until required. Serve the chicken kabobs with the raita, lemon wedges, boiled rice, and a crisp salad.

PICTURED RIGHT.

NUTRITION FACTS	
Serving size 1 (362g)	
Calories 332 Calories from fat 54	
	% daily value*
Total fat 6g	9%
Saturated fat 2g	8%
Cholesterol 122mg	41%
Sodium 364mg	15%
Total carbohydrate 19g	6%
Dietary fiber 3g	11%
Sugars 13g	0%
Protein 49g	0%

*Percent daily values are based on a 2,000-calorie diet

garlic chicken

Don't be put off by the amount of garlic in this recipe. The garlic is baked unpeeled and is used for flavor only, like the bunches of herbs which are also used. Dedicated garlic lovers may want to spread some of the cooked garlic purée onto lightly toasted French bread to eat with the chicken.

❖

one 3½-lb oven-ready chicken
2 sprigs each of parsley, tarragon, rosemary, and thyme
2 bay leaves
2 tsp coarse sea salt
black pepper
40 cloves garlic, unpeeled
1 Tbsp fennel seeds
fresh herbs, to garnish

❖

PREPARATION TIME / 5 MINUTES
COOKING TIME / 1 HOUR 30 MINUTES
serves 4

Presoak the claypot as directed. Wash the chicken, inside and out, and pat dry using paper towels, then place in the pot.

Take a sprig of each herb and a bay leaf and tie together in a bunch with string. Repeat with the remaining herbs and bay leaf. Place one bunch inside the chicken cavity, and the other in the pot. Rub the salt and pepper all over the chicken. Scatter in the garlic and sprinkle over the fennel seeds. Cover and place in a cold oven. Set the oven to 425° and cook for 1½ hours until the chicken is tender and thoroughly cooked – the juices will run clear when the bird is done.

Discard the herbs and place the chicken on a serving platter. Surround with some of the baked garlic. Garnish with herbs and serve with toasted French bread.

NUTRITION FACTS	
Serving size 1 (431g)	
Calories 977 Calories from fat 477	
	% daily value*
Total fat 53g	81%
Saturated fat 15g	74%
Cholesterol 421mg	140%
Sodium 1968mg	82%
Total carbohydrate 11g	4%
Dietary fiber 1g	3%
Sugars 0g	0%
Protein 108g	0%

*Percent daily values are based on a 2,000-calorie diet

oriental chicken drumsticks

A popular party or buffet dish, these spicy chicken drumsticks can be eaten hot or cold. Allow a little extra time for marinating to ensure the best flavor.

❖

8 medium-sized chicken drumsticks, skinned

3 Tbsp dark soy sauce

½ tsp hot chili powder

1 tsp Chinese five-spice powder

one 1-inch piece ginger root, peeled and grated

1 garlic clove, peeled and minced

1 Tbsp clear honey

1 tsp sesame oil

1 Tbsp sesame seeds

4 scallions, trimmed and finely shredded

red chile strips to garnish

❖

PREPARATION TIME / 15 MINUTES PLUS MARINATING
COOKING TIME / 1 HOUR

serves 4

Wash and pat dry the chicken drumsticks using paper towels. Using a small sharp knife score each chicken drumstick in a crisscross design on the fleshy part. Place in a shallow dish. Mix together the soy sauce, chili, and five-spice powder, ginger root, garlic, honey, and sesame oil. Pour over the chicken, cover, and chill for 2 hours.

Presoak the claypot as directed, and line the bottom with waxed paper. Drain the chicken and arrange in the pot. Spoon over the marinade, cover, and place in a cold oven. Set oven to 425° and cook for 45 minutes.

Sprinkle with the sesame seeds and cook, uncovered, for a further 15 minutes, until tender and done. Serve hot or cold, sprinkled with shredded scallions, and garnished with red chile.

PICTURED LEFT.

NUTRITION FACTS	
Serving size 1 (127g)	
Calories 211 Calories from fat 72	
	% daily value*
Total fat 8g	12%
Saturated fat 2g	8%
Cholesterol 82mg	27%
Sodium 863mg	36%
Total carbohydrate 8g	3%
Dietary fiber 1g	3%
Sugars 5g	0%
Protein 26g	0%
*Percent daily values are based on a 2,000-calorie diet	

chicken and sausage pot

You can still enjoy sausages on a low-fat diet by choosing a low-fat variety or those made with minced turkey or chicken. Here the simplest of ingredients are enhanced with wine and mushrooms.

❖

8 slim low-fat sausages

8 chicken thighs, skinned

1 tbsp cornstarch

4 large field mushrooms, peeled and sliced

8 oz assorted mushrooms such as shiitake, open cup or button, wiped and halved or quartered

2 garlic cloves, peeled and minced

1 bouquet garni

salt and black pepper

1 cup dry red wine

2 Tbsp chopped parsley

❖

PREPARATION TIME / 10 MINUTES

cooking time / 1 hour 18 minutes

serves 4

Presoak the claypot as directed. Preheat the broiler to a hot setting. Arrange the sausages on the broiler and cook for 2–3 minutes on each side to brown. Drain on paper towels. Wash and pat dry the chicken thighs. Dust with cornstarch and set aside.

Place the sliced and assorted mushrooms in the base of the claypot and sprinkle over the garlic. Push the bouquet garni in amongst the mushrooms. Arrange the chicken and sausages over the mushrooms and pour over the wine. Season well. Cover and place in a cold oven. Set the oven to 450° and cook for 1 hour 30 minutes until the chicken is done. Discard the bouquet garni and serve sprinkled with chopped parsley. Accompany with bread to mop up the gravy.

NUTRITION FACTS	
Serving size 1 (393g)	
Calories 490 Calories from fat 162	
	% daily value*
Total fat 18g	27%
Saturated fat 5g	26%
Cholesterol 169mg	56%
Sodium 1204mg	50%
Total carbohydrate 21g	7%
Dietary fiber 1g	4%
Sugars 6g	0%
Protein 53g	0%
*Percent daily values are based on a 2,000-calorie diet	

boned chicken with peach stuffing

Succulent chicken with a sweet, nutty filling is baked with fragrant peaches and carves easily into slices. It may be served hot, or cold as part of a buffet.

❖

one 4-lb chicken, cleaned and boned
salt and black pepper
½ cup low-fat soft cheese flavored with garlic and herbs
¼ cup dry white breadcrumbs
2 Tbsp chopped parsley
1 bunch scallions, trimmed and finely chopped
¼ cup no-soak dried peaches, finely chopped
3 Tbsp pecans, finely chopped
3 Tbsp peach chutney
1 large egg, beaten
5 ripe peaches
¼ cup dry white wine
sprigs of parsley, to garnish

❖

PREPARATION TIME / 30 MINUTES
COOKING TIME / 1 HOUR 30 MINUTES
serves 8

Presoak the claypot as directed. Open out the chicken, then place it flesh side up on a clean surface. Season the inside of the chicken.

Mix together the soft cheese, breadcrumbs, chopped parsley, scallions, dried peaches, and pecans. Season well and bind together with the chutney and egg to form a firm mixture. Pile the stuffing into the center of the chicken, fold over to form a roll, then secure using skewers. Place the chicken in the claypot.

Wash and dry the peaches, and halve and pit one peach. Cut into thin wedges and arrange around and over the chicken. Cover and place in a cold oven. Set the oven to 425° and cook for 1 hour 15 minutes.

Just before the end of the cooking time, halve and pit the remaining peaches. Place the peach halves around the chicken, and spoon over the wine. Continue to cook, uncovered, for a further 15 minutes until the chicken is tender and the juices run clear. Discard the skewers. Serve hot or cold, in slices, garnished with the peaches and parsley.

PICTURED RIGHT.

NUTRITION FACTS	
Serving size 1 (328g)	
Calories 538 Calories from fat 189	
	% daily value*
Total fat 21g	32%
Saturated fat 6g	32%
Cholesterol 235mg	78%
Sodium 392mg	16%
Total carbohydrate 14g	5%
Dietary fiber 2g	8%
Sugars 8g	0%
Protein 70g	0%

*Percent daily values are based on a 2,000-calorie diet

chicken with bananas and corn

The unusual combination of spicy and sweet flavors make this dish a mouthwatering meal. The amount of chile you add will depend on your personal taste. Serve with mashed potatoes and a crisp salad.

❖

4 corn cobs, trimmed and cut into 2-inch pieces
1–2 green chiles, deseeded and finely chopped
¼ cup golden raisins
2 Tbsp white wine vinegar
1 tsp ground cinnamon
1 Tbsp light brown sugar
1 cup fresh chicken broth
four 8-oz chicken quarters, skinned
4 rindless bacon slices, trimmed and cut lengthways into 4 thin strips
salt and black pepper
2 firm medium bananas
1 Tbsp lemon juice

❖

PREPARATION TIME / 15 MINUTES
COOKING TIME / 1 HOUR 30 MINUTES
serves 4

Presoak the claypot as directed. Arrange the corn in pieces in the base of the pot and sprinkle over the chiles, raisins, and vinegar. Dust with the cinnamon and brown sugar, then pour over the broth.

Wash and pat dry the chicken quarters using paper towels. Wrap four strips of bacon around each chicken quarter in a crisscross design. Place the chicken quarters on top of the corn and season generously. Cover and place in a cold oven. Set the oven to 425° and cook for 1¼ hours.

Just before the end of cooking, peel and thickly slice the bananas. Toss in the lemon juice to prevent browning. Add to the pot, cover, and cook for a further 10–15 minutes until the bananas have just softened.

NUTRITION FACTS	
Serving size 1 (453g)	
Calories 575 Calories from fat 108	
	% daily value*
Total fat 12g	19%
Saturated fat 4g	19%
Cholesterol 198mg	66%
Sodium 705mg	29%
Total carbohydrate 39g	13%
Dietary fiber 3g	13%
Sugars 21g	0%
Protein 76g	0%

*Percent daily values are based on a 2,000-calorie diet

stuffed turkey cutlets with marsala

Turkey cutlets make a tasty alternative to veal. Here they are stuffed and rolled on a bed of bell peppers in Marsala wine.

❖

2 red bell peppers, deseeded and thinly sliced
2 yellow bell peppers, deseeded
and thinly sliced
2 orange bell peppers, deseeded
and thinly sliced
6 oz shallots, peeled and shredded
¾ cup fresh turkey or chicken broth
¾ cup Marsala
four 5-oz thin turkey breast fillets
½ cup low-fat soft cheese flavored with garlic
and herbs
4 slices Parma ham
1 Tbsp cornstarch
8 large basil leaves
salt and black pepper
3 Tbsp pitted black olives in brine,
drained and sliced
shredded basil, to garnish

❖

PREPARATION TIME / 20 MINUTES
COOKING TIME / 1 HOUR 25 MINUTES
serves 4

Presoak the claypot as directed. Place the bell peppers and shallots in the bottom of the pot. Mix well and pour over the broth and wine. Cover and place in a cold oven. Set the oven to 425° and cook for 40 minutes.

Meanwhile, place the turkey between two sheets of waxed paper and beat them out thinly with a meat mallet. Peel off the paper and spread with the soft cheese. Top with a slice of ham, then roll up tightly. Dust with the cornstarch. Fold two large basil leaves around the outside of each then secure the rolls with cocktail sticks and place on the peppers and shallots. Season well.

Place the turkey on top of the peppers, cover, and cook for 30 minutes. Remove the lid and cook for a further 15 minutes until tender and done. Remove cocktail sticks. Serve each roll thinly sliced and fanned out on a bed of peppers. Sprinkle with olives and shredded basil to garnish.

PICTURED RIGHT.

NUTRITION FACTS	
Serving size 1 (600g)	
Calories 429 Calories from fat 72	
	% daily value*
Total fat 8g	12%
Saturated fat 4g	20%
Cholesterol 137mg	46%
Sodium 657mg	27%
Total carbohydrate 30g	10%
Dietary fiber 1g	6%
Sugars 6g	0%
Protein 52g	0%
*Percent daily values are based on a 2,000-calorie diet	

turkey with apples and peanuts

This is an excellent way to use up leftover cooked turkey. The flavor is sweet and mildly curried. Pile onto cooked rice or use as a filling for baked potatoes.

❖

1 large red onion, peeled and finely chopped
2 apples, peeled and cored, and each cut into
8 wedges
2 Tbsp lemon juice
2 stalks celery, trimmed and chopped
1 tbsp mild curry powder
2 bay leaves
1 cup fresh turkey or chicken broth
salt and black pepper
3 Tbsp cornstarch
2 cups skim milk
2 Tbsp crunchy peanut butter
1¼ cups diced, cooked turkey
½ cup frozen peas, thawed
3 Tbsp roasted salted peanuts, crushed

❖

PREPARATION TIME / 10 MINUTES
COOKING TIME / 1 HOUR 20 MINUTES
serves 4

Presoak the claypot as directed. Place the red onion and apple in the bottom and toss in the lemon juice. Mix in the celery, curry powder, and bay leaves.

Pour over the broth, season well, cover, and place in a cold oven. Set the oven to 425° and cook for 1 hour, stirring occasionally.

Twenty minutes before the end of cooking, blend the cornstarch with a little of the milk to form a paste and set aside. Spoon the peanut butter into a saucepan and gradually blend in the remaining milk. Bring to a boil, stirring, until very thick, then set aside with a layer of plastic wrap over the surface to prevent a skin forming.

Spoon the peanut sauce over the vegetables and gently blend together with the broth and vegetables. Stir in the turkey and peas. Cover and cook for a further 15 minutes until heated through. Discard the bay leaves and check the seasoning. Serve sprinkled with chopped peanuts.

NUTRITION FACTS	
Serving size 1 (415g)	
Calories 343 Calories from fat 81	
	% daily value*
Total fat 9g	14%
Saturated fat 2g	9%
Cholesterol 73mg	24%
Sodium 605mg	25%
Total carbohydrate 30g	10%
Dietary fiber 4g	17%
Sugars 16g	0%
Protein 36g	0%
*Percent daily values are based on a 2,000-calorie diet	

oriental roast duck

Duck is a very fatty bird, but most of the fat is found in and just beneath the skin, so it is easily removed before eating. In this recipe the duck is basted with Chinese spices and seasonings for maximum flavor.

one 5-lb duckling, giblets removed
4 Tbsp dark soy sauce
2 Tbsp light brown sugar
2 garlic cloves, peeled and minced
one 1-inch piece ginger root, peeled and grated
1 tsp Szechuan peppercorns, crushed
1 tsp Chinese five-spice powder

for the dip
2 Tbsp dark soy sauce
2 Tbsp rice wine or sweet sherry
2 scallions, trimmed and finely shredded
pinch of Chinese five-spice powder

to serve
pancakes
shredded cucumber and scallions

PREPARATION TIME / 10 MINUTES PLUS CHILLING
COOKING TIME / 1 HOUR 45 MINUTES
serves 4

Wash and dry the duckling using paper towels. Trim away the excess skin and fat. Prick the skin all over with a fork and place the duck in a shallow dish. Mix together the remaining ingredients for the duckling and spoon over. Cover and chill for 2 hours, basting occasionally.

Presoak the claypot as directed. Drain the duckling and place in the claypot. Spoon over the marinade. Cover and place in a cold oven. Set the oven to 425° and cook for 1 hour 45 minutes, or until the duck is done and the juices run clear. After 1 hour of cooking, discard as much fat and juice as possible.

To serve, mix all the dip ingredients together and place in a small serving bowl. Drain the duck well, and then strip away all the skin and fat. Shred the flesh. Diners choose some duck, roll it up in pancakes, add pieces of cucumber and scallions, and dip in the soy dip.

PICTURED LEFT.

NUTRITION FACTS	
Serving size 1 (720g)	
Calories 2474 Calories from fat 2016	
	% daily value*
Total fat 224g	345%
Saturated fat 75g	376%
Cholesterol 431mg	144%
Sodium 1912mg	80%
Total carbohydrate 38g	13%
Dietary fiber 1g	3%
Sugars 7g	0%
Protein 70g	0%

*Percent daily values are based on a 2,000-calorie diet

duck with pears and pecans

Duck on the bone lends itself particularly well to claypot cooking. The richness of the meat in this recipe is balanced by the pears. There is added flavor and spice from the orange and cinnamon.

four 6-oz duck portions, skinned
1 large orange
1 cinnamon stick, broken
2 bay leaves
salt and black pepper
4 ripe pears
1 Tbsp lemon juice
3 Tbsp pecan halves, slivered
1 tsp ground cinnamon
orange slices and chopped parsley, to garnish

PREPARATION TIME / 10 MINUTES
COOKING TIME / 1 HOUR
serves 4

Presoak the claypot as directed. Wash and pat dry the duck portions with paper towels and place in the pot.

Using a vegetable peeler, pare some of the rind from the orange and add a few strips to the duck. Extract the juice and pour over. Add the cinnamon stick and bay leaves, and season well. Cover and place in a cold oven. Set the oven to 425° and cook for 40 minutes.

Just before the end of cooking, peel, core, and quarter the pears and toss in the lemon juice to prevent browning. Carefully push the pears under the duck, cover, and cook for a further 15–20 minutes until the duck is done and the pears are tender.

Discard the orange rind, cinnamon stick, and bay leaves. Serve dusted with ground cinnamon and garnished with orange slices and parsley.

NUTRITION FACTS	
Serving size 1 (403g)	
Calories 504 Calories from fat 207	
	% daily value*
Total fat 23g	36%
Saturated fat 7g	37%
Cholesterol 151mg	50%
Sodium 260mg	11%
Total carbohydrate 34g	11%
Dietary fiber 7g	26%
Sugars 22g	0%
Protein 42g	0%

*Percent daily values are based on a 2,000-calorie diet

duck with plum stuffing and apples

This is a tangy mixture of rich meat and sharp fruits. Serve this dish with Chinese plum sauce, noodles, and stir-fried green vegetables. This is an impressive dinner-party dish.

❖

4 dessert apples

1 Tbsp lemon juice

2 Tbsp superfine sugar

four 6-oz boneless duck breasts, skinned

½ cup cooked rice

2 medium plums, pitted and chopped

one ½-inch piece ginger root, peeled and finely chopped

1 Tbsp chopped chives

salt and black pepper

4 Tbsp dry sherry

chives and slices of plum, to garnish

❖

PREPARATION TIME / 15 MINUTES

COOKING TIME / 1 HOUR 5 MINUTES

serves 4

Presoak the claypot as directed. Peel, core and thickly slice the apples into rings. Place in the claypot and sprinkle with lemon juice and four teaspoons sugar. Set aside.

Wash and pat dry the duck breasts with paper towels. Using a small sharp knife, make a slit through the side of each, taking care not to cut through the top or bottom, to make a deep pocket in each.

Mix together the rice, plums, ginger, and chives and season well. Spoon the rice stuffing into each pocket, and press together gently to seal. Secure with cocktail sticks.

Place the duck breasts on top of the apple rings. Spoon over the sherry and the remaining sugar and season again. Cover and place in a cold oven. Set the oven to 450° and cook for 50 minutes. Remove the lid and cook, uncovered, for a further 15 minutes. To serve, drain the duck and arrange apple rings on warmed serving plates. Top with a piece of duck and sprinkle with chopped chives and plum slices. Accompany with noodles and stir-fried green vegetables.

NUTRITION FACTS	
Serving size 1 (499g)	
Calories 444 Calories from fat 108	
	% daily value*
Total fat 12g	18%
Saturated fat 4g	21%
Cholesterol 131mg	44%
Sodium 272mg	11%
Total carbohydrate 52g	17%
Dietary fiber 6g	23%
Sugars 33g	0%
Protein 33g	0%

*Percent daily values are based on a 2,000-calorie diet

pheasant with root vegetables

Pheasant is an increasingly popular game bird. The flesh is rich and benefits from being cooked with some sweet ingredients. In this dish, the pheasants are baked with sweet root vegetables and maple syrup.

❄

1 lb carrots, peeled and thickly sliced

1 lb parsnips, peeled and thickly sliced

1 Tbsp all-purpose flour

a few bay leaves

2 Tbsp maple syrup

¾ cup fresh vegetable broth

salt and black pepper

2 pheasants, plucked and drawn, each weighing approximately 1½ lb

4 slices bacon, trimmed

parsley and bay leaves, to garnish

❄

PREPARATION TIME / **20 MINUTES**

COOKING TIME / **1 HOUR 48 MINUTES**

serves 4

Place the carrots and parsnips in a large saucepan and cover with water. Bring to a boil and boil for 6–8 minutes. Drain well, return to the saucepan, and add the flour. Allow to cool.

Meanwhile, presoak the claypot as directed. Transfer the cooled root vegetables to the pot and push the bay leaves in among them. Spoon over the maple syrup and pour over the broth. Season.

Wipe the pheasants and pat dry with paper towels. Truss the birds by tying their legs together with clean string. Cut each bacon slice widthways in half and place over the pheasants. Place the pheasants on top of the root vegetables. Cover and place in a cold oven. Set the oven to 400° and cook for 1½ hours. Remove the lid and bake for a further 10 minutes, depending on their size, until they are tender and done, and the juices run clear.

Discard the bacon and place the pheasants on a warmed serving platter. Drain the root vegetables and discard the bay leaves. Arrange the vegetables around the pheasants. Garnish with parsley and bay leaves. Carve and serve, removing the skin before eating. Serve accompanied by white gravy and green vegetables.

NUTRITION FACTS		
Serving size 1 (628g)		
Calories 668 Calories from fat 144		
		% daily value*
Total fat 16g		25%
Saturated fat 5g		27%
Cholesterol 230mg		77%
Sodium 440mg		18%
Total carbohydrate 43g		14%
Dietary fiber 8g		33%
Sugars 14g		0%
Protein 85g		0%

*Percent daily values are based on a 2,000-calorie diet

pheasant with cranberries

Cranberries add a tartness to any dish and they are a perfect foil for game. The mixture of sweet spices and fruit in this recipe makes this an excellent choice for a Christmas meal.

◧

1 lb red cabbage, shredded

1 large red onion, peeled and shredded

2 Tbsp red wine vinegar

¼ cup golden raisins

1 cup cranberries, thawed if frozen

½ cup light brown sugar

1 cinnamon stick, broken

6 whole cloves

6 cardamom pods, split

1 cup dry red wine

four 5-oz boneless pheasant breasts, skinned

salt and black pepper

4 slices bacon, trimmed

1 small orange

wedges of orange and fresh herbs, to garnish

◧

PREPARATION TIME / 10 MINUTES

COOKING TIME / 1 HOUR

serves 4

Presoak the claypot as directed. Place the red cabbage and onion in the base of the pot and mix in the vinegar to coat. Add the raisins, cranberries, sugar, and spices. Mix well. Pour over the red wine and set aside.

Wash and pat dry the pheasant breasts with paper towels. Season on both sides. Cut the bacon into thin lengthways strips and wrap around each breast.

Using a vegetable peeler, pare off four pieces of orange rind and carefully tuck a piece under the bacon.

Place the pheasant breasts on top of the cabbage mixture. Extract the orange juice and spoon over the pheasant. Cover and place in a cold oven. Set the oven to 425° and cook for 1 hour until tender and done.

Remove the pheasant breasts and discard the orange rind if preferred. Drain the cabbage and discard the spices. Pile onto warmed serving plates and top each with a pheasant breast. Garnish and serve with green vegetables and cranberry sauce.

NUTRITION FACTS		
Serving size 1 (443g)		
Calories 472	Calories from fat 72	
		% daily value*
Total fat 8g		13%
Saturated fat 3g		14%
Cholesterol 88mg		29%
Sodium 323mg		13%
Total carbohydrate 52g		18%
Dietary fiber 5g		22%
Sugars 40g		0%
Protein 39g		0%

*Percent daily values are based on a 2,000-calorie diet

meat

meatballs with ratatouille sauce

Tender morsels of seasoned beef are baked in a rich and colorful sauce of Mediterranean vegetables. They are ideal served with pasta, rice or couscous.

❖

1 lb extra-lean ground beef
2 slices white bread, made into breadcrumbs
1 small onion, peeled and finely chopped
1 garlic clove, peeled and minced
2 Tbsp chopped parsley
salt and black pepper
1 medium egg, beaten

for the ratatouille sauce

1 large onion, peeled and finely chopped
1 medium red bell pepper, deseeded and diced
1 medium yellow bell pepper, deseeded and diced
1 large zucchini, trimmed and diced
1 medium eggplant, trimmed and diced
two 14-oz cans chopped tomatoes
2 tsp superfine sugar
1 bouquet garni

❖

PREPARATION TIME / 15 MINUTES
COOKING TIME / 1 HOUR 15 MINUTES
serves 4

Presoak the claypot as directed. Place the beef, onion, garlic, parsley, seasoning, and egg in a bowl and mix well together. Form into 16 balls. Set aside.

Place the vegetables in the claypot and stir in the canned tomatoes and sugar. Season well. Push the bouquet garni into the mixture. Arrange the meatballs on top of the vegetables. Cover and place in a cold oven. Set the oven to 425° and cook for 1 hour. Remove the lid and cook for a further 15 minutes until tender.

Discard the bouquet garni and serve the meatballs and sauce with pasta, rice or couscous.

NUTRITION FACTS	
Serving size 1 (576g)	
Calories 412 Calories from fat 198	
	% daily value*
Total fat 22g	34%
Saturated fat 8g	42%
Cholesterol 123mg	41%
Sodium 324mg	14%
Total carbohydrate 29g	10%
Dietary fiber 6g	24%
Sugars 13g	0%
Protein 28g	0%

*Percent daily values are based on a 2,000-calorie diet

beef enchiladas

Enchilada, a Spanish–American word meaning "filled with chili," is a tortilla folded around a mixture of meat, cheese, chili, and other ingredients, which is then baked in a rich tomato sauce.

❧

2 medium onions, peeled and chopped
1 large green bell pepper, deseeded and chopped
1 garlic clove, peeled and minced
2 celery stalks, trimmed and chopped
1 lb extra-lean ground beef
½–1 tsp chili powder
1 Tbsp ground cumin
two 14-oz cans chopped tomatoes
salt and black pepper
1 Tbsp vegetable oil
12 tortillas
¼ cup pitted black olives in brine, drained
2 Tbsp chopped cilantro
½ cup grated low-fat Cheddar cheese
2 jalapeño peppers, chopped

❧

PREPARATION TIME / 15 MINUTES
COOKING TIME / 1 HOUR 15 MINUTES
serves 4

Presoak the claypot as directed. Place the onion, bell pepper, garlic, celery, beef, chili powder, cumin, and ½ can of tomatoes in the pot. Season and mix well. Cover and place in a cold oven. Set the oven to 425° and cook for 50 minutes, stirring occasionally.

Just before the end of cooking, brush a nonstick skillet with some oil and fry each tortilla for a few seconds on each side until blistered. Drain on paper towels. Pour the remaining tomatoes onto a plate and dip the fried tortillas in the mixture to soften slightly.

Working quickly, spread two tablespoons cooked beef mixture onto each tortilla in a lengthways central strip. Fold both sides over the beef and roll slightly. Place seam-side down back in the pot.

Pour the remainder of the tomatoes from the plate over the enchiladas. Sprinkle with olives, cilantro, cheese, and jalapeño peppers. Cover and bake for a further 25 minutes until hot and bubbling. Serve the enchiladas with a crisp green salad.

PICTURED LEFT.

NUTRITION FACTS	
Serving size 1 (588g)	
Calories 892 Calories from fat 315	
	% daily value*
Total fat 35g	54%
Saturated fat 11g	54%
Cholesterol 88mg	29%
Sodium 1437mg	60%
Total carbohydrate 100g	33%
Dietary fiber 10g	40%
Sugars 2g	0%
Protein 48g	0%
*Percent daily values are based on a 2,000-calorie diet	

corn beef hash with beetroot

More familiar versions of this dish are simply a combination of potato and corn beef. In this dish, diced beetroot is added for extra color and flavor. Serve with plain yogurt spooned over.

❧

1 lb potatoes, peeled and diced
1 lb beetroot, peeled and finely diced
1 large onion, peeled and finely chopped
2 Tbsp all-purpose flour
salt and black pepper
¾ cup fresh vegetable broth
1 lb cooked corn beef, finely chopped
4 Tbsp chopped parsley
6 Tbsp plain yogurt
1 tsp paprika

❧

PREPARATION TIME / 10 MINUTES
COOKING TIME / 1 HOUR 20 MINUTES
serves 6

Presoak the claypot as directed. Place the potatoes, beetroot, onion, and flour in the pot. Mix well. Season well and pour over the broth. Cover and place in a cold oven. Set the oven to 425° and cook for 1 hour, stirring occasionally.

Stir in the corn beef. Mix well and return to the oven. Cook, uncovered, for a further 20 minutes, stirring after 10 minutes. Stir in the chopped parsley and then spoon on to warmed serving plates. Top each with a spoonful of yogurt and sprinkle with a little paprika.

NUTRITION FACTS	
Serving size 1 (280g)	
Calories 239 Calories from fat 45	
	% daily value*
Total fat 5g	7%
Saturated fat 2g	10%
Cholesterol 36mg	12%
Sodium 862mg	36%
Total carbohydrate 27g	9%
Dietary fiber 2g	7%
Sugars 2g	0%
Protein 21g	0%
*Percent daily values are based on a 2,000-calorie diet	

meatloaf with spinach stuffing

Meatloaf is a classic family favorite. This version is rolled up like a jelly roll and has a delicious nutmeg-flavored spinach spiral running through it. Serve with tomato sauce.

1 medium onion, peeled and finely chopped

1 garlic clove, peeled and minced

2 lb extra-lean ground beef

salt and black pepper

breadcrumbs, made from 4 slices white bread

2 medium eggs

10 oz frozen chopped spinach, drained

½ tsp ground nutmeg

for the sauce

1 cup puréed tomatoes, sieved

½ cup dry white wine or fresh vegetable broth

2 Tbsp tomato paste

1 tsp superfine sugar

1 tsp dried onion granules

1 tsp dried mixed herbs

PREPARATION TIME / 25 MINUTES PLUS STANDING

COOKING TIME / 1 HOUR 30 MINUTES

serves 4

Presoak the claypot as directed and line the bottom with waxed paper. Place the onion, garlic, ground beef, seasoning, breadcrumbs, and the eggs in a bowl. Mix well to form a firm mixture.

Lay a sheet of waxed paper onto the work surface and spread the beef mixture into a 14 x 8-inch rectangle.

Press the spinach with the back of a spoon against the sides of a strainer to extract as much water as possible. Place in a bowl and mix in the nutmeg and some seasoning. Spread the spinach over the meat, keeping it 1 inch away from the end.

Starting at the narrow end, roll up the beef like a jelly roll, using the waxed paper to help you, and loosening the beef with a spatula if necessary. Press together then discard the paper. Carefully transfer to the pot. Cover and place in a cold oven. Set the oven to 400° and bake for 1½ hours until the loaf is done. Allow to stand for 15 minutes.

Meanwhile, place all the ingredients for the sauce in a saucepan and heat through, stirring, until hot. Carefully remove the loaf from the claypot and place on a warmed serving plate. Slice and serve with the sauce.

NUTRITION FACTS	
Serving size 1 (451g)	
Calories 703 Calories from fat 378	
	% daily value*
Total fat 42g	65%
Saturated fat 16g	82%
Cholesterol 249mg	83%
Sodium 612mg	26%
Total carbohydrate 23g	8%
Dietary fiber 4g	16%
Sugars 4g	0%
Protein 51g	0%

*Percent daily values are based on a 2,000-calorie diet

beef tamale pie

In Mexico, tamales consist mainly of maize dough with a little meat and some sauce. This baked dish has a crisp topping of cheese cornbread.

❧

2 garlic cloves, peeled and minced

1 orange bell pepper, deseeded and diced

2 stalks celery, trimmed and chopped

1 lb extra-lean ground beef

1¼ cups sweetcorn kernels

1 cup canned kidney beans, drained and rinsed

one 14-oz can chopped tomatoes

½–1 tsp chili powder

salt and black pepper

2 Tbsp chopped cilantro

for the topping

½ cup cornmeal

1 Tbsp all-purpose flour

½ tsp salt

2 tsp baking powder

1 medium egg, beaten

6 Tbsp skim milk

1 Tbsp corn oil

¼ cup grated low-fat Cheddar cheese

❧

PREPARATION TIME / 10 MINUTES

COOKING TIME / 1 HOUR 10 MINUTES

serves 4

Presoak the claypot as directed. Place the garlic, bell pepper, celery, beef, sweetcorn, and kidney beans in the pot and mix well. Add the tomatoes, chili, and seasoning. Cover and place in a cold oven. Set the oven to 425° and cook for 45 minutes, stirring occasionally.

Just before the end of cooking, mix together the cornmeal, flour, salt, and baking powder. Make a well in the center, add the egg, milk, and oil and beat well to form a smooth batter.

Stir the chopped cilantro into the beef mixture. Spoon the cornbread mixture roughly over the top and sprinkle with cheese. Cook, uncovered, for a further 25 minutes until golden and firm. Serve straight from the pot.

PICTURED LEFT.

NUTRITION FACTS	
Serving size 1 (456g)	
Calories 514 Calories from fat 243	
	% daily value*
Total fat 27g	41%
Saturated fat 9g	46%
Cholesterol 129mg	43%
Sodium 1051mg	44%
Total carbohydrate 34g	12%
Dietary fiber 7g	28%
Sugars 6g	0%
Protein 36g	0%
*Percent daily values are based on a 2,000-calorie diet	

beef pot roast with vegetables

A pot roast is always comforting on a cold day. Chuck steak cooks to a meltingly tender texture in the claypot, turning an economical cut into a very tasty meal.

❧

2 large onions, peeled and thickly sliced

4 medium carrots, peeled and thickly sliced

6 medium potatoes, peeled and halved

1 bouquet garni

½ tsp ground nutmeg

2½ cups fresh beef broth

one 3-lb piece chuck steak

4 slices bacon, trimmed

salt and black pepper

1 Tbsp cornstarch

2 Tbsp chopped parsley

❧

PREPARATION TIME / 15 MINUTES

COOKING TIME / 2 HOURS 15 MINUTES

serves 6

Presoak the claypot as directed. Place the onions, carrot and potatoes in the pot and mix well. Push in the bouquet garni and sprinkle over the nutmeg. Pour in the broth.

Wash and pat dry the beef with paper towels. Season all over. Slice the bacon lengthways into thin strips and arrange over the beef. Tie up the meat into a neat shape using clean string. Place over the vegetables, cover, and place in a cold oven. Set the oven to 425° and cook for 2¼ hours until tender.

Transfer the meat to a warmed serving platter. Remove the vegetables using a slotted spoon and arrange around the beef. Cover and set aside.

Meanwhile, strain the juice into a saucepan. Discard the bouquet garni. Blend the cornstarch with two tablespoons cold water and stir into the broth. Heat, stirring, until thickened. Pour the thickened broth into a warmed jug. Discard the string from the beef and press the chopped parsley over the top. Slice and serve.

NUTRITION FACTS	
Serving size 1 (504g)	
Calories 1028 Calories from fat 369	
	% daily value*
Total fat 41g	63%
Saturated fat 16g	82%
Cholesterol 136mg	45%
Sodium 436mg	19%
Total carbohydrate 79g	26%
Dietary fiber 4g	16%
Sugars 5g	0%
Protein 43g	0%
*Percent daily values are based on a 2,000-calorie diet	

beef stifadho

A traditional Greek and Cypriot dish, this rich casserole of beef and onions cooked in tomatoes and spices is delicious served on a bed of hot bulgur wheat or boiled rice.

◈

1 Tbsp vegetable oil

1½ lb lean chuck steak, cubed

12 oz baby onions, peeled and kept whole

4 garlic cloves, peeled and minced

3 bay leaves

10 black peppercorns

1 stick of cinnamon, broken

4 Tbsp red wine vinegar

1 Tbsp superfine sugar

two 14-oz cans chopped tomatoes

2 Tbsp tomato paste

1 tsp salt

2 Tbsp chopped parsley

◈

PREPARATION TIME / 15 MINUTES

COOKING TIME / 2 HOURS 15 MINUTES

serves 4

Presoak the claypot as directed. Heat the oil in a large skillet and fry the beef, onions, and garlic for 4–5 minutes until the beef is browned all over. Allow to cool for 10 minutes.

Transfer the beef to the claypot and add the bay leaves, peppercorns, and cinnamon. Spoon over the vinegar and sugar. Mix well.

Pour over the tomatoes and tomato paste and season with salt. Carefully mix in. Cover and place in a cold oven. Set the oven to 400° and cook for 2 hours, until tender.

Remove the lid and cook for a further 10 minutes. Discard the bay leaves and spices. Check the seasoning and serve sprinkled with chopped parsley.

NUTRITION FACTS	
Serving size 1 (505g)	
Calories 518 Calories from fat 180	
	% daily value*
Total fat 20g	31%
Saturated fat 6g	32%
Cholesterol 140mg	47%
Sodium 760mg	32%
Total carbohydrate 24g	8%
Dietary fiber 6g	23%
Sugars 13g	0%
Protein 61g	0%

*Percent daily values are based on a 2,000-calorie diet

spiced beef with port gravy

Spiced beef is a traditional English Christmas dish. Tender beef fillet with a lemon and parsley stuffing, wrapped in lean bacon, bakes perfectly in a claypot and makes a mouthwatering, luxurious meal.

☜

one 3-lb piece beef fillet, trimmed
½ cup ruby port
4 Tbsp red wine vinegar
2 Tbsp dark brown sugar
1 tsp ground allspice
8 slices bacon, trimmed
1 tsp finely grated lemon rind
1 Tbsp lemon juice
2 Tbsp fresh chopped parsley
½ tsp salt
½ cup fresh white breadcrumbs
1 medium egg, beaten
1 cup fresh beef broth
1 Tbsp cornstarch
lemon wedges and sprigs of parsley,
to garnish

☜

PREPARATION TIME / **20 MINUTES PLUS OVERNIGHT MARINATING**
COOKING TIME / **1 HOUR 45 MINUTES**
serves 8

First prepare the beef. Using a sharp knife, slice down the center of the beef lengthways, to within 1 inch of the other side. Open out the beef and pound it with a meat mallet to tenderize it. Transfer to a shallow dish and pour over the port and vinegar. Sprinkle with the sugar and allspice. Chill overnight, turning occasionally.

The next day, presoak the claypot as directed. Finely chop two slices of bacon and mix with lemon rind, juice, parsley, salt, and breadcrumbs. Bind together with the egg to form a stuffing. Drain the beef, reserving the marinade, and spread the stuffing down the center of the beef. Roll up and wrap the remaining bacon over the length of the beef. Secure with clean string. Transfer the beef to the claypot. Cover and place in a cold oven. Set the oven to 400° and cook for 1½–1¾ hours, until done to your liking.

Just before the end of cooking, blend the reserved marinade with the cornstarch and place in a saucepan. Pour in the broth and heat through, stirring, until thickened. Check the seasoning. Transfer the beef to a warmed serving plate, discard the string, and serve hot with the port gravy. Garnish and accompany with a selection of vegetables of your choice. Alternatively, allow the beef to cool and serve sliced as part of a buffet.

NUTRITION FACTS

Serving size 1 (245g)
Calories 557 Calories from fat 144

	% daily value*
Total fat 16g	25%
Saturated fat 6g	31%
Cholesterol 180mg	60%
Sodium 449mg	19%
Total carbohydrate 24g	8%
Dietary fiber 0g	2%
Sugars 4g	0%
Protein 55g	0%

*Percent daily values are based on a 2,000-calorie diet

roast lamb with a curried crust

This lamb dish benefits from a yogurt crust which encases the meat and keeps it very moist and tender. The curry spices used here create a fragrant flavor, rather than a hot one.

〜

one 4-lb leg of lamb
1 cup plain yogurt
one 1-inch piece ginger root, peeled and chopped
4 garlic cloves, peeled and minced
1 medium onion, peeled and chopped
1 fresh green chile, deseeded and chopped
1 Tbsp ground coriander
1 tsp ground cumin
1 tsp garam masala
1 tsp ground turmeric
1 tsp salt
2 Tbsp canned coconut milk
small bunch of cilantro, to garnish

〜

PREPARATION TIME / 10 MINUTES PLUS OVERNIGHT MARINATING
COOKING TIME / 1 HOUR 50 MINUTES
serves 6

Remove as much fat as possible from the lamb and lay it on a board. Using a small sharp knife, make deep incisions all over the lamb – make them as deep as possible, trying to slice to the bone. Place the lamb in a deep dish and set aside.

Placed all the remaining ingredients except the bunch of cilantro for garnish in a blender and blend until smooth. Alternatively, finely chop the ginger, garlic, onion, and chile and mix with the other ingredients to form a paste. Spoon the spiced yogurt mixture over the lamb and spread well all over the surface. Cover the dish and chill overnight, turning occasionally.

The next day, presoak the claypot as directed and line with waxed paper. Transfer the lamb to the pot, cover, and place in a cold oven. Set the oven to 425° and cook for 1 hour 50 minutes or until done to your liking.

Place the lamb on a serving platter, and sprinkle over the roughly shredded cilantro. Serve with Indian relishes, rice, and a salad.

PICTURED LEFT.

NUTRITION FACTS	
Serving size 1 (357g)	
Calories 625 Calories from fat 225	
	% daily value*
Total fat 25g	39%
Saturated fat 9g	47%
Cholesterol 270mg	90%
Sodium 627mg	26%
Total carbohydrate 6g	2%
Dietary fiber 1g	2%
Sugars 2g	0%
Protein 89g	0%
*Percent daily values are based on a 2,000-calorie diet	

lamb kleftiko with sweet red onions

Traditionally made with lamb or young goat, this Greek dish must be made in a sealed pot for the best results. In Cyprus, Kleftiko is made in a special claypot and cooked in a small oven in the backyard.

〜

one 4-lb leg of lamb
3 large red onions, peeled and cut into 8 wedges
2 Tbsp lemon juice
1 Tbsp superfine sugar
1 tsp salt
black pepper
1 tsp chopped oregano
1 tsp chopped thyme
2 large tomatoes, deseeded and chopped
4 bay leaves
fresh herbs, to garnish

〜

PREPARATION TIME / 10 MINUTES
COOKING TIME / 1 HOUR 50 MINUTES
serves 6

Presoak the claypot as directed. Trim away fat from the lamb. Place the onions in the pot and sprinkle with the lemon juice, sugar, salt, pepper, oregano, and thyme. Place the lamb on top. Cover and place in a cold oven. Set the oven to 425° and cook for 1 hour.

Spoon the tomatoes under and around the lamb. Add the bay leaves and season again. Cover and continue to cook for a further 50 minutes until the lamb is tender and cooked to your liking. Drain the lamb and vegetables, discard the bay leaves, and arrange on a warmed serving platter. Garnish with herbs.

NUTRITION FACTS	
Serving size 1 (367g)	
Calories 604 Calories from fat 216	
	% daily value*
Total fat 24g	36%
Saturated fat 8g	42%
Cholesterol 269mg	90%
Sodium 652mg	27%
Total carbohydrate 7g	2%
Dietary fiber 1g	3%
Sugars 4g	0%
Protein 86g	0%
*Percent daily values are based on a 2,000-calorie diet	

rack of lamb with a mustard crust

A popular and impressive dish to serve when entertaining, rack of lamb is tender and sweet. In this recipe, the sweetness is enhanced with a honey mustard crust and redcurrant sauce.

◇

½ cup fresh white breadcrumbs
3 Tbsp wholegrain mustard
2 Tbsp clear honey
1 Tbsp olive oil
2 Tbsp chopped fresh rosemary or 2 tsp dried
salt and black pepper
three 14-oz prepared racks of lamb,
with 6 rib chops on each
redcurrants and sprigs of rosemary to garnish

for the sauce
4 Tbsp redcurrant jelly
5 Tbsp red wine vinegar
1 Tbsp chopped fresh rosemary or 1 tsp dried

◇

PREPARATION TIME / 10 MINUTES
COOKING TIME / 1 HOUR 10 MINUTES
serves 6

Presoak the claypot as directed and line with waxed paper. First make the crust. Mix the breadcrumbs, mustard, honey, oil, rosemary, and seasoning together to form a stuffing.

Trim away any excess fat from the lamb. Press the stuffing onto the meaty side of the lamb racks and place in the pot, stacking them side by side, overlapping. Cover and place in a cold oven. Set the oven to 425° and cook for 1 hour. Remove the lid and bake for a further 10 minutes or until done to your liking.

Meanwhile, make the sauce. Place the redcurrant jelly in a small saucepan and heat gently until melted. Stir in the vinegar and rosemary. Set aside to cool.

Remove the lamb from the pot and place on a warmed serving platter. Garnish and serve with the sauce.

PICTURED RIGHT.

NUTRITION FACTS	
Serving size 1 (249g)	
Calories 644 Calories from fat 432	
	% daily value*
Total fat 48g	74%
Saturated fat 20g	100%
Cholesterol 143mg	48%
Sodium 371mg	15%
Total carbohydrate 14g	5%
Dietary fiber 1g	3%
Sugars 7g	0%
Protein 36g	0%
*Percent daily values are based on a 2,000-calorie diet	

lamb with flageolet beans

This is a hearty, satisfying dish of tender lamb cooked on a bed of beans. Flageolet beans, slim and pale green in color, are very popular in France and go very well with lamb. Haricot beans would also be suitable.

◇

1 cup dried flageolet beans, soaked overnight
salt and black pepper
2 garlic cloves, peeled and minced
8 oz shallots, peeled and left whole
2 large tomatoes, seeded and chopped
2 sprigs rosemary
1 cup fresh vegetable broth
four 10-oz chump chops or lamb shanks
sprigs of rosemary, to garnish

◇

PREPARATION TIME / 10 MINUTES PLUS OVERNIGHT SOAKING
COOKING TIME / 2 HOURS 30 MINUTES
serves 4

Presoak the claypot as directed. Drain and rinse the beans and place in a saucepan. Cover with water, bring to a boil, and boil rapidly for 10 minutes. Drain and rinse under cold running water. Cool for 10 minutes.

Transfer the beans to the pot and add the garlic, shallots, and tomatoes. Mix well. Push the rosemary sprigs into the mixture. Pour over the broth and season well, cover, and place in a cold oven. Set the oven to 425° and cook for 2 hours, stirring occasionally.

Just before the end of cooking time, trim as much fat from the lamb as possible and season well on both sides. Mix the bean mixture and then place the lamb on top of the beans, cover, and bake for 30 minutes until the lamb is tender. Discard the rosemary sprigs. Spoon the beans and lamb onto warmed serving plates, garnish with rosemary, and serve with French bread.

NUTRITION FACTS	
Serving size 1 (522g)	
Calories 785 Calories from fat 171	
	% daily value*
Total fat 19g	29%
Saturated fat 6g	31%
Cholesterol 295mg	98%
Sodium 401mg	17%
Total carbohydrate 48g	16%
Dietary fiber 1g	3%
Sugars 4g	0%
Protein 103g	0%
*Percent daily values are based on a 2,000-calorie diet	

hawaiian pork chops

Add interest to simple pork chops with this recipe where they are cooked with fresh pineapple and vegetable rice.

❖

1 red bell pepper, deseeded and chopped
1 green bell pepper, deseeded and chopped
1 medium onion, peeled and chopped
4 medium tomatoes, peeled, deseeded, and chopped
1 tsp dried mixed herbs
3 Tbsp chopped parsley
1¼ cups long-grain rice, washed
3½ cups vegetable broth
salt and black pepper
four 6-oz boneless pork chops
½ medium-ripe pineapple, peeled, cored, and diced
1 tsp ground paprika
sprigs of parsley, to garnish

❖

PREPARATION TIME / 15 MINUTES
COOKING TIME / 1 HOUR 15 MINUTES
serves 4

Presoak the claypot as directed. Place the bell peppers, onion, tomatoes, herbs, parsley, and rice in the pot. Mix well and pour over the broth. Season well. Cover and place in a cold oven. Set the oven to 425° and cook for 30 minutes.

Meanwhile, trim as much fat from the chops as possible and season on both sides. Place the chops on top of the rice and scatter the pineapple on top. Cover and cook for a further 30 minutes.

Remove the lid and bake for a further 15 minutes until the pork is done and the rice has absorbed all the liquid.

Spoon onto a warmed serving plate and sprinkle with ground paprika. Garnish and serve.

PICTURED LEFT.

NUTRITION FACTS	
Serving size 1 (731g)	
Calories 520 Calories from fat 135	
	% daily value*
Total fat 15g	23%
Saturated fat 5g	26%
Cholesterol 140mg	47%
Sodium 423mg	18%
Total carbohydrate 40g	13%
Dietary fiber 4g	17%
Sugars 15g	0%
Protein 56g	0%
*Percent daily values are based on a 2,000-calorie diet	

pork pot roast with lemon and juniper

A moist roast of tender lean pork stuffed with crisp water chestnuts. Serve the meat in slices with freshly cooked vegetables, and the thickened cooking juices as a sauce or gravy.

❖

¼ cup cooked white and wild rice
¼ cup canned water chestnuts, drained and chopped
4 scallions, trimmed and chopped
1 tsp finely grated lemon rind
1 Tbsp lemon juice
2 Tbsp chopped chives
salt and black pepper
one 3-lb boneless pork shoulder
½ cup dry vermouth
1 cup fresh vegetable broth
4 juniper berries, crushed
1 Tbsp cornstarch
lemon slices and chives, to garnish

❖

PREPARATION TIME / 15 MINUTES
COOKING TIME / 2 HOURS
serves 6

Presoak the claypot as directed. Mix together the rice, water chestnuts, scallions, lemon rind, lemon juice, chives, and seasoning. Set aside.

Trim away the rind and fat from the pork. Push the stuffing into the cavity where the bone was, and then place in the claypot. Add the vermouth, broth, and berries. Cover and place in a cold oven. Set the oven to 425° and cook for 2 hours until done.

Drain the pork and place on a warmed platter. Strain the cooking liquor into a saucepan, and discard the juniper berries. Blend the cornstarch with two tablespoons water and add to the liquor. Heat through, stirring, until thickened. Season. Serve the pork garnished with lemon slices and chives, and accompany with the gravy.

NUTRITION FACTS	
Serving size 1 (335g)	
Calories 592 Calories from fat 279	
	% daily value*
Total fat 31g	48%
Saturated fat 11g	54%
Cholesterol 205mg	68%
Sodium 286mg	12%
Total carbohydrate 12g	4%
Dietary fiber 1g	4%
Sugars 4g	0%
Protein 58g	0%
*Percent daily values are based on a 2,000-calorie diet	

chinese red pork

Marinating tender, lean pork in a blend of dark soy sauce and Chinese seasonings gives this dish its red color. Serve in thin slices, with vegetable garnishes, and extra soy sauce for dipping.

one 1½-lb pork loin tenderloin
4 Tbsp dark soy sauce
2 Tbsp rice wine or sweet sherry
1 tsp Chinese five-spice powder
2 garlic cloves, peeled and minced
one 1-inch ginger root, peeled and finely chopped

for the glaze

¼ cup superfine sugar
4 Tbsp sherry vinegar

to serve

scallion tassels
carrot and red bell pepper triangles
dark soy sauce for dipping

PREPARATION TIME / 10 MINUTES PLUS MARINATING
COOKING TIME / 1 HOUR 30 MINUTES
serves 4

Trim any excess fat and membrane from the pork and place in a shallow dish. Mix together the soy sauce, wine or sherry, five-spice powder, garlic, and ginger. Pour over the pork, cover, and chill overnight, turning occasionally.

The next day, presoak the claypot as directed and line the base with waxed paper. Drain the pork, reserving the marinade, and place in the pot. Brush generously with the marinade, cover, and place in cold oven. Set the oven to 400° and cook for 1 hour. Brush with more marinade and cook, uncovered, for a further 20–30 minutes until tender and done, basting occasionally.

Just before the end of cooking, prepare the glaze. Place the sugar and vinegar in a small saucepan and heat gently to melt the sugar. Bring to a boil and simmer for 3–4 minutes, until a syrupy consistency is reached.

As soon as the pork is cooked, remove it from the pot and place on a wire rack. Brush with the glaze and leave to stand for 5 minutes. Slice the pork thinly and arrange the slices on a warmed serving platter. Garnish and serve with soy sauce for dipping.

NUTRITION FACTS	
Serving size 1 (290g)	
Calories 351 Calories from fat 81	
	% daily value*
Total fat 9g	13%
Saturated fat 3g	14%
Cholesterol 134mg	45%
Sodium 1647mg	69%
Total carbohydrate 13g	4%
Dietary fiber 1g	4%
Sugars 7g	0%
Protein 51g	0%

*Percent daily values are based on a 2,000-calorie diet

spicy spareribs

Spareribs are a popular dish. Because they are often eaten with the fingers, don't forget to put finger bowls of water and lemon on the table with some napkins.

❖

3 lb meaty pork spareribs
1 medium onion, peeled and finely chopped
2 garlic cloves, peeled and minced
1 Tbsp light brown sugar
2 Tbsp red wine vinegar
2 Tbsp Worcestershire sauce
½ cup catsup
3 Tbsp tomato paste
½ tsp celery salt
1 tsp chili sauce (optional)
salt and black pepper
orange wedges and fresh parsley, to garnish

❖

PREPARATION TIME / 10 MINUTES
COOKING TIME / 1 HOUR 20 MINUTES
serves 4

Presoak the claypot as directed and line the bottom with waxed paper. Trim away the excess fat from the ribs then place them in the pot.

Mix together the remaining ingredients, except the garnish, and brush generously all over the ribs. Cover and place in a cold oven. Set the oven to 425° and cook for 1 hour, turning halfway through. Remove the lid and cook for a further 20 minutes, until the ribs are tender and a rich, reddish-brown color.

Remove from the pot and pile onto a warmed serving platter. Garnish and serve with barbecue relish.

PICTURED RIGHT.

NUTRITION FACTS	
Serving size 1 (469g)	
Calories 1171 Calories from fat 837	
	% daily value*
Total fat 93g	143%
Saturated fat 37g	184%
Cholesterol 208mg	69%
Sodium 871mg	36%
Total carbohydrate 22g	8%
Dietary fiber 1g	5%
Sugars 14g	0%
Protein 58g	0%

*Percent daily values are based on a 2,000-calorie diet

maple-roasted ham with apricots

An impressive dish which can be served hot or cold as part of a buffet. The fruit and maple syrup helps to counteract the saltiness of the ham.

❖

one 3-lb picnic ham, boned and rolled
1 onion, peeled and quartered
2 stalks celery, trimmed and cut into large pieces
1 carrot, peeled and roughly chopped
2 bay leaves
1 Tbsp black peppercorns
2 Tbsp whole cloves
4 Tbsp apricot chutney
4 Tbsp maple syrup
1 Tbsp wholegrain mustard
1 cup no-soak dried apricots
½ cup dry sherry
bay leaves, to garnish

❖

PREPARATION TIME / 15 MINUTES
COOKING TIME / 2 HOURS
serves 6-8

Place the ham in a large saucepan. Add the onion, celery, carrot, bay leaves, and peppercorns. Cover with cold water, bring to a boil, and skim away the surface scum. Cover and simmer for 1 hour.

Presoak the claypot as directed and line the bottom with waxed paper. Drain the ham, discarding the vegetables, bay leaves, and peppercorns, and strip away the brown skin and most of the white fat, leaving only a thin layer.

Score the fat in diamond shapes and press a whole clove into each divided section. Mix together the chutney, maple syrup, and mustard and brush generously over the ham fat. Transfer the ham to the pot and arrange the apricots around.

Pour in the sherry, cover, and place in a cold oven. Set the oven to 425° and cook for 1 hour until tender. Serve, garnished with bay leaves, with the apricots as an accompaniment.

NUTRITION FACTS	
Serving size 1 (281g)	
Calories 438 Calories from fat 99	
	% daily value*
Total fat 11g	17%
Saturated fat 4g	18%
Cholesterol 107mg	36%
Sodium 2630mg	110%
Total carbohydrate 28g	9%
Dietary fiber 3g	12%
Sugars 21g	0%
Protein 50g	0%

*Percent daily values are based on a 2,000-calorie diet

mixed grill

A delicious meal that would serve as a hearty brunch. Choose lean cuts of meat for this recipe in order to keep the fat content as low as possible, and look out for low-fat sausages.

❖

4 large low-fat sausages
four 3-oz lean lamb cutlets, trimmed
4 bacon slices, about ¼ inch thick, trimmed
1 large baking potato, scrubbed and cut into thin wedges
4 large flat mushrooms, peeled and thickly sliced
4 medium onions, peeled and quartered
4 beefsteak tomatoes, quartered
1 Tbsp chopped fresh thyme or 1 tsp dried
salt and black pepper
½ cup fresh vegetable broth
1 Tbsp wholegrain mustard
1 tsp dried rosemary
sprigs of thyme and rosemary, to garnish

❖

PREPARATION TIME / 15 MINUTES
COOKING TIME / 1 HOUR 20 MINUTES
serves 4

Presoak the claypot as directed. Preheat the broiler to a hot setting. Place the sausages, lamb, and ham on the broiler rack and place under the heat for 2–3 minutes on each side to brown. Drain on paper towels.

Place the potatoes in the bottom of the pot and top with the mushrooms, onions, and tomatoes. Sprinkle with the thyme and season well. Pour in the broth.

Place the sausages on top of the vegetables. Spread the mustard over the ham and sprinkle the lamb with the rosemary. Place on top of the vegetables. Cover and place in a cold oven. Set the oven to 450° and cook for 1 hour 10 minutes, turning the meat over halfway through. Remove the lid and cook, uncovered, for a further 10 minutes.

Drain the vegetables and divide between warmed serving plates. Top each with a sausage, a cutlet, and a slice of ham. Garnish and serve.

PICTURED RIGHT.

NUTRITION FACTS	
Serving size 1 (398g)	
Calories 394 Calories from fat 135	
	% daily value*
Total fat 15g	23%
Saturated fat 5g	25%
Cholesterol 119mg	40%
Sodium 864mg	36%
Total carbohydrate 24g	8%
Dietary fiber 2g	10%
Sugars 7g	0%
Protein 41g	0%

*Percent daily values are based on a 2,000-calorie diet

sweet and sour venison meatballs

Venison is now widely available ground and makes a good, lower-fat substitute for ground beef, pork, and lamb in all manner of dishes. Serve these meatballs with noodles or pasta.

❖

1 lb ground venison
½ cup cooked white and wild rice
1 medium leek, trimmed and finely chopped
½ cup canned sweetcorn kernels, drained
2 tsp Chinese five-spice powder
salt and black pepper
1 large egg, beaten
1 large green bell pepper, deseeded and sliced
1 large red bell pepper, deseeded and sliced
1 large yellow bell pepper, deseeded and sliced
6 oz kumquats, thinly sliced
1 Tbsp superfine sugar
1 cup unsweetened orange juice
1 cup fresh vegetable broth
2 Tbsp cornstarch
chopped chives and shredded leek, to garnish

❖

PREPARATION TIME / 15 MINUTES
COOKING TIME / 1 HOUR 15 MINUTES
serves 4

Presoak the claypot as directed. Place the venison in a bowl and add the rice, leek, sweetcorn, five-spice powder, and seasoning. Bind together with the beaten egg.

Divide the mixture into 20 and form into balls. Set aside. Place the bell peppers in the pot along with the kumquats. Sprinkle with the sugar and seasoning. Pour over the orange juice and mix well.

Top with the meatballs, cover, and place in a cold oven. Set the oven to 425° and cook for 1 hour. Remove the lid and cook, uncovered for a further 15 minutes.

Drain the meatballs and peppers using a slotted spoon, and transfer to a warmed serving platter. Pour the cooking liquid into a saucepan. Blend a little of the broth with the cornstarch and add to the saucepan along with the remaining broth. Heat through, stirring, until thickened. Check the seasoning.

Spoon the sauce over the meatballs and garnish to serve.

NUTRITION FACTS	
Serving size 1 (502g)	
Calories 398 Calories from fat 54	
	% daily value*
Total fat 6g	10%
Saturated fat 2g	11%
Cholesterol 189mg	63%
Sodium 658mg	27%
Total carbohydrate 43g	14%
Dietary fiber 5g	21%
Sugars 11g	0%
Protein 43g	0%

*Percent daily values are based on a 2,000-calorie diet

venison and prune stew

A rich game meat that is naturally lean and low in fat. This rich combination of tender venison chunks cooked in red wine with assorted vegetables and soft prunes is delicious served with garlic-flavored mashed potatoes.

⬡

1½ lb lean stewing venison, cut into 1-inch cubes

2 Tbsp all-purpose flour

salt and black pepper

1 tsp dried mixed herbs

8 oz shallots, peeled

2 large carrots, peeled and diced

2 stalks celery, trimmed and chopped

1 cup mushrooms, wiped and halved

2 garlic cloves, peeled and minced

1 bouquet garni

1 cup dry red wine

1 cup fresh beef broth

2 Tbsp redcurrant jelly

¾ cup no-soak dried prunes

2 Tbsp chopped parsley, to garnish

⬡

PREPARATION TIME / **15 MINUTES**

COOKING TIME / **2 HOURS 10 MINUTES**

serves 4

Presoak the claypot as directed. Place the venison in a bowl and add the flour, seasoning, and mixed herbs. Toss well to coat the venison in the flour mixture.

Place the shallots, carrots, celery, mushrooms, and garlic in the pot and mix well. Top with the venison, and push the bouquet garni into the vegetables. Pour over the red wine, broth, and add the redcurrant jelly. Carefully mix well together. Top with the prunes and season well. Cover and place in a cold oven. Set the oven to 400° and cook for 2 hours. Remove the lid and cook, uncovered, for a further 10 minutes.

Serve the venison on warmed serving plates, sprinkled with chopped parsley.

NUTRITION FACTS	
Serving size 1 (460g)	
Calories 510 Calories from fat 63	

	% daily value*
Total fat 7g	11%
Saturated fat 3g	13%
Cholesterol 205mg	68%
Sodium 1096mg	46%
Total carbohydrate 42g	14%
Dietary fiber 4g	17%
Sugars 19g	0%
Protein 60g	0%

*Percent daily values are based on a 2,000-calorie diet

vegetables and vegetarian dishes

middle eastern-style stuffed vegetables

This assortment of vegetables makes a filling lunch or supper dish, or an interesting accompaniment to a casserole or stew.

✧

3 cups cooked white rice

2 oz golden raisins

3 Tbsp toasted pine nuts

1 Tbsp finely chopped red onion

4 Tbsp lemon juice

2 Tbsp chopped cilantro

1 tsp ground cinnamon

1 tsp ground coriander

salt and black pepper

1 large egg, beaten

2 medium orange bell peppers

2 medium zucchini

4 baby eggplants

1 large tomato, skinned, deseeded, and chopped

sprigs of cilantro, to garnish

✧

PREPARATION TIME / 15 MINUTES

COOKING TIME / 50 MINUTES

serves 4

Presoak a large claypot as directed and line the bottom with waxed paper. In a bowl, mix the rice, raisins, pine nuts, red onion, and one tablespoon lemon juice. Add the chopped cilantro, cinnamon, and ground coriander. Season well and bind together with the egg. Set aside.

Halve and deseed the peppers. Trim and halve the zucchini lengthways and scoop out the central flesh. Chop this flesh and add to the stuffing. Trim and halve the eggplants, and scoop out the central flesh. Chop this flesh and add to the stuffing.

Sprinkle the vegetables with the remaining lemon juice, season, and then fill each with stuffing mixture. Place the vegetables in the pot, cover, and place in a cold oven. Set the oven to 450° and cook for 50 minutes or until tender.

Serve the vegetables topped with a little chopped tomato and a few sprigs of cilantro.

NUTRITION FACTS	
Serving size 1 (449g)	
Calories 350	Calories from fat 63
	% daily value*
Total fat 7g	10%
Saturated fat 1g	6%
Cholesterol 53mg	18%
Sodium 184mg	8%
Total carbohydrate 67g	22%
Dietary fiber 4g	17%
Sugars 14g	0%
Protein 10g	0%

*Percent daily values are based on a 2,000-calorie diet

cauliflower and broccoli cheese bake

This baked dish of cauliflower and broccoli florets in a flavorful cheese sauce makes a perfect vegetarian main course.

◈

12 oz cauliflower florets

12 oz broccoli florets

½ cup vegetable broth

3 cups skim milk

2 Tbsp cornstarch

1 large egg yolk

3 Tbsp chopped chives

½ cup grated low-fat Cheddar cheese

salt and black pepper

2 Tbsp fresh white breadcrumbs

1 Tbsp grated Parmesan cheese

chives, to garnish

◈

PREPARATION TIME / 10 MINUTES

COOKING TIME / 35 MINUTES

serves 4

Presoak a small claypot as directed. Bring a saucepan of water to a boil and blanch the cauliflower and broccoli for 1 minute. Drain well and rinse under cold running water to cool. Pat dry using paper towels and place in the claypot. Pour over the broth, cover, and place in a cold oven. Set the oven to 425° and cook for 20 minutes.

Halfway through cooking, in a saucepan, blend a little of the milk with the cornstarch to form a paste, and then stir in the remaining milk. Bring to a boil, stirring, until very thick. Remove from the heat and stir in the egg yolk, chives, and Cheddar. Season well.

Working quickly, using a slotted spoon, remove the vegetables and place in a heatproof bowl. Carefully blend the sauce into the cooking liquid and return the vegetables to the pot. Gently mix in the sauce.

Mix the breadcrumbs and Parmesan cheese together and sprinkle over the top. Return to the oven and cook, uncovered, for 15 minutes until crisp and golden. Serve sprinkled with chopped chives.

PICTURED RIGHT.

NUTRITION FACTS

Serving size 1 (426g)

Calories 224   Calories from fat 54

	% daily value*
Total fat 6g	9%
Saturated fat 2g	11%
Cholesterol 68mg	23%
Sodium 427mg	18%
Total carbohydrate 24g	8%
Dietary fiber 5g	19%
Sugars 12g	0%
Protein 22g	0%

*Percent daily values are based on a 2,000-calorie diet

sweetcorn bake

Juicy sweetcorn kernels, baked in milk and flavored with a hint of nutmeg, make an unusual accompaniment to ham or bacon.

◈

2 large eggs

1½ tsp salt

1 tsp superfine sugar

black pepper

2 cups skim milk

1¼ cups canned or frozen sweetcorn kernels, drained or defrosted

½ tsp grated nutmeg

3 Tbsp freshly grated Parmesan cheese

2 Tbsp chopped parsley

◈

PREPARATION TIME / 5 MINUTES

COOKING TIME / 1 HOUR 10 MINUTES

serves 4

Presoak the claypot as directed. Place the eggs in a mixing bowl. Add the salt, sugar, and pepper and beat together. Gradually whisk in the milk and stir in the sweetcorn. Transfer to the claypot and sprinkle with the nutmeg. Cover and set the oven to 375° and bake for 1 hour.

Remove the lid, sprinkle with the cheese, if using, and cook, uncovered, for a further 10 minutes until set or until a knife inserted in the center comes out clean. Sprinkle with the chopped parsley to serve.

NUTRITION FACTS

Serving size 1 (208g)

Calories 145   Calories from fat 36

	% daily value*
Total fat 4g	7%
Saturated fat 2g	9%
Cholesterol 111mg	37%
Sodium 1147mg	48%
Total carbohydrate 17g	6%
Dietary fiber 1g	5%
Sugars 8g	0%
Protein 10g	0%

*Percent daily values are based on a 2,000-calorie diet

twice-baked potatoes in their jackets

Choose a variety of potato with a floury texture for best results. This dish is filling enough to make a tasty supper or light lunch, but is an excellent accompaniment to any meal.

four 8-oz medium baking potatoes, scrubbed
½ cup soft cheese flavored with garlic and herbs
4 scallions, trimmed and shredded
½ tsp powdered mustard
salt and black pepper
1 medium egg, beaten
2 Tbsp grated Parmesan cheese
2 slices cooked bacon, crumbled (optional)
2 Tbsp chopped chives

PREPARATION TIME / 15 MINUTES
COOKING TIME / 1 HOUR 45 MINUTES
serves 4

Presoak the claypot as directed and line the bottom with waxed paper. Prick the potatoes all over using a fork and place in the pot. Cover and place in a cold oven. Set the oven to 450° and cook for 1 hour 30 minutes or until tender.

With a sharp knife, carefully slice the potatoes in half lengthways. With a spoon, carefully scoop out all the potato flesh, taking care not to damage the skin, and place in a mixing bowl. Reserve the potato shells. Add the soft cheese to the potato flesh and mash together. Stir in the scallions, mustard, and seasoning. Keeping a little egg back for glazing, beat in the remainder of the egg to form a smooth consistency.

Pile the mashed potato back into the potato shells. Brush with egg and sprinkle with Parmesan cheese. Return to the claypot and cook, uncovered, for a further 15 minutes.

Serve sprinkled with crumbled bacon, if using, and chopped chives.

NUTRITION FACTS		
Serving size 1 (275g)		
Calories 389	Calories from fat 126	
		% daily value*
Total fat 14g		21%
Saturated fat 8g		38%
Cholesterol 76mg		25%
Sodium 361mg		15%
Total carbohydrate 58g		19%
Dietary fiber 5g		22%
Sugars 4g		0%
Protein 11g		0%
*Percent daily values are based on a 2,000-calorie diet		

boston baked beans

A Puritan Boston dish made by the womenfolk on Saturday, and then served on Sunday when no cooking was allowed. The original recipe includes salt pork. This is a vegetarian version and should be served with bread to mop up the sauce.

꙰

1 lb navy beans, soaked overnight
1 Tbsp dry mustard
1 Tbsp molasses
¼ cup dark brown sugar
sprig of fresh thyme
sprig of fresh rosemary
1 bay leaf
4 Tbsp tomato paste
2 cups fresh vegetable broth
salt and black pepper
1 large onion, peeled
4 cloves
sprigs of thyme to garnish

꙰

PREPARATION TIME / 10 MINUTES
COOKING TIME / 2 HOURS 10 MINUTES
serves 6

Presoak the claypot as directed. Drain the beans and rinse under cold water. Place in a large saucepan and cover with water. Bring to a boil and boil rapidly for 10 minutes. Drain and rinse again. Cool for 10 minutes.

Transfer to the pot and mix in the mustard, molasses, and sugar. Tie the herbs together with a clean piece of string and push into the beans. Mix the tomato paste into the broth and pour over the beans. Season well. Stud the onion with the cloves and push into the center of the beans. Cover and place in a cold oven. Set the oven to 400° and cook for 1 hour 45 minutes. Stir and cook, uncovered, for a further 15 minutes until rich and tender.

Discard the herbs and onion. Garnish and serve with bread.

NUTRITION FACTS	
Serving size 1 (166g)	
Calories 111	Calories from fat 9
	% daily value*
Total fat 1g	1%
Saturated fat 0g	0%
Cholesterol 0mg	0%
Sodium 185mg	8%
Total carbohydrate 23g	8%
Dietary fiber 3g	10%
Sugars 12g	0%
Protein 3g	0%

*Percent daily values are based on a 2,000-calorie diet

sweetcorn curry

This dish is not only simple to prepare, but when served with some rice, Indian pickles, and chutneys, becomes a dish fit for a maharaja!

꙰

1 large onion, peeled and finely chopped
1-inch piece ginger root, peeled and grated
2 large potatoes, peeled and finely diced
1 large green bell pepper, deseeded and chopped
2 garlic cloves, peeled and finely chopped
2 bay leaves
2 tsp mild curry powder
4 Tbsp canned coconut milk
1 cup fresh vegetable broth
1 lb canned sweetcorn kernels, drained
salt and black pepper
4 Tbsp cilantro

꙰

PREPARATION TIME / 5 MINUTES
COOKING TIME / 1 HOUR 15 MINUTES
serves 4

Presoak a claypot as directed. Place the onion, ginger, potatoes, bell pepper, and garlic in the pot, and mix well. Push in the bay leaves.

Mix together the curry powder, coconut milk, and broth and pour into the pot. Cover and place in a cold oven. Set oven to 425° and cook for 1 hour, stirring occasionally, until tender.

Stir in the sweetcorn and season well. Cover and cook for a further 15 minutes, stirring halfway through, until hot. Discard the bay leaves. Stir in the cilantro and serve, accompanied with rice.

NUTRITION FACTS	
Serving size 1 (383g)	
Calories 282	Calories from fat 45
	% daily value*
Total fat 5g	8%
Saturated fat 3g	17%
Cholesterol 0mg	0%
Sodium 862mg	36%
Total carbohydrate 57g	19%
Dietary fiber 6g	26%
Sugars 8g	0%
Protein 7g	0%

*Percent daily values are based on a 2,000-calorie diet

italian-style stuffed squash

Butternut squash have a sweet, earthy flavor and a bright orange-yellow flesh. They make a stunning vegetable accompaniment because of their unusual long shape.

❧

2 tsp olive oil

1 medium red onion, peeled and chopped

1 Tbsp lemon juice

2 garlic cloves, peeled and minced

2 small butternut squash

salt and black pepper

3 cups cooked rice

2 large tomatoes, peeled, deseeded, and chopped

¼ cup pitted black olives in brine, drained and chopped

1 small bunch basil, shredded

3 Tbsp grated Parmesan cheese

basil leaves, to garnish

❧

PREPARATION TIME / 10 MINUTES

COOKING TIME / 1 HOUR

serves 4

Presoak a large claypot as directed. Heat the oil in a small saucepan. Add the onion, lemon juice, and garlic and fry gently for 3–4 minutes until just softened. Transfer to a mixing bowl to cool.

Meanwhile, cut the squash in half lengthways. Scoop out the fiber and seeds from the center and season well. Mix the rice, tomatoes, olives, and shredded basil into the cooked onion mixture. Season well and pile into the prepared squash.

Arrange in the claypot, cover, and place in a cold oven. Set the oven to 425° and cook for 45 minutes. Remove the lid, sprinkle with the cheese, and cook for a further 15 minutes, until crisp and golden. Garnish with basil leaves to serve.

PICTURED RIGHT.

NUTRITION FACTS	
Serving size 1 (293g)	
Calories 282	Calories from fat 54
	% daily value*
Total fat 6g	9%
Saturated fat 1g	6%
Cholesterol 3mg	1%
Sodium 330mg	14%
Total carbohydrate 52g	17%
Dietary fiber 2g	7%
Sugars 4g	0%
Protein 6g	0%

*Percent daily values are based on a 2,000-calorie diet

potato and leek gratin

This recipe uses baby new potatoes which have a firmer texture. You can use larger varieties if you prefer, but they are better peeled. Try serving this dish with baked ham or roast chicken.

❧

2 large leeks, trimmed, washed and shredded

4 slices rindless bacon, trimmed and chopped (optional)

2 Tbsp chopped chives

1½ lb baby new potatoes, scrubbed and thinly sliced

salt and black pepper

1 cup skim milk

1 Tbsp butter, melted

chives and shredded leek, to garnish

❧

PREPARATION TIME / 10 MINUTES

COOKING TIME / 1 HOUR 15 MINUTES

serves 4

Presoak a small claypot as directed. Layer half the leeks, bacon if using, chives, and potatoes in the pot and season well. Top with the remaining vegetables, finishing with a layer of potatoes; season again and pour over the milk.

Cover the pot and place in a cold oven. Set the oven to 425°. Cook for 1 hour, then brush with the melted butter and cook, uncovered, for a further 15 minutes until tender and golden brown. Garnish with chives and shredded leeks before serving.

NUTRITION FACTS	
Serving size 1 (306g)	
Calories 258	Calories from fat 63
	% daily value*
Total fat 7g	10%
Saturated fat 3g	16%
Cholesterol 15mg	5%
Sodium 332mg	14%
Total carbohydrate 42g	14%
Dietary fiber 4g	15%
Sugars 5g	0%
Protein 9g	0%

*Percent daily values are based on a 2,000-calorie diet

bulgur wheat pilaf

Bulgur wheat is a staple in the Middle East and is the essential ingredient of Tabbouleh. It has a nutty flavor and is ideal served with pitta bread and hummous as a light lunch or supper dish. It also makes an excellent accompaniment to a spicy stew.

❖

1 cup bulgur wheat

1 Tbsp ground coriander

3 cups fresh vegetable broth

2 large tomatoes, peeled, deseeded, and chopped

2 medium zucchini, trimmed and coarsely grated

¼ cup golden raisins

2 Tbsp chopped mint

2 Tbsp chopped parsley

2 Tbsp chopped cilantro

4 Tbsp lemon juice

1 Tbsp olive oil

salt and black pepper

3 Tbsp toasted pine nuts

1 small lemon, cut into wedges

fresh herbs, to garnish

❖

PREPARATION TIME / 10 MINUTES PLUS STANDING
COOKING TIME / 1 HOUR 5 MINUTES
serves 4

Presoak the claypot as directed. Place the bulgur wheat in the pot. Stir in the ground coriander and broth. Cover and place in a cold oven. Set the oven to 450° and cook for 45 minutes, stirring occasionally, until soft and tender.

Stir in the tomatoes, zucchini, and raisins. Cover and cook for a further 20 minutes. Add the herbs, lemon juice, olive oil, and seasoning after standing for 10 minutes.

Sprinkle with the pine nuts. Serve with lemon wedges, and garnished with fresh herbs.

PICTURED LEFT.

NUTRITION FACTS	
Serving size 1 (472g)	
Calories 354 Calories from fat 81	
	% daily value*
Total fat 9g	14%
Saturated fat 1g	6%
Cholesterol 0mg	0%
Sodium 310mg	13%
Total carbohydrate 64g	21%
Dietary fiber 12g	46%
Sugars 12g	0%
Protein 10g	0%
*Percent daily values are based on a 2,000-calorie diet	

baked eggs with bell peppers

Based on a Tunisian dish called Chakchouka, which is made in a skillet on top of the stove, this dish of baked sweet bell peppers flavored with chili and topped with eggs makes an interesting and unusual lunch dish.

❖

1 large onion, peeled and shredded

2 red bell peppers, deseeded and shredded

2 yellow bell peppers, deseeded and shredded

one 14-oz can chopped tomatoes

1 tsp chili powder

1 tsp superfine sugar

salt and black pepper

4 large eggs

2 Tbsp chopped mint

❖

PREPARATION TIME / 10 MINUTES
COOKING TIME / 1 HOUR 15 MINUTES
serves 4

Presoak the claypot as directed. Place the onion, bell peppers, tomatoes, chili, sugar, and seasoning in the pot and mix well. Cover and place in a cold oven. Set the oven to 425° and cook for 1 hour.

Remove the lid and make four small indentations in the bell pepper mixture. Break an egg into each and cook, uncovered, for a further 10–15 minutes until the eggs have cooked to your liking. Serve straight from the pot, sprinkled with chopped mint.

NUTRITION FACTS	
Serving size 1 (413g)	
Calories 171 Calories from fat 54	
	% daily value*
Total fat 6g	9%
Saturated fat 2g	8%
Cholesterol 212mg	71%
Sodium 230mg	10%
Total carbohydrate 22g	7%
Dietary fiber 4g	17%
Sugars 8g	0%
Protein 10g	0%
*Percent daily values are based on a 2,000-calorie diet	

wilted lettuce with lemon dressing

Lettuces need not be used in salads; try this recipe and bake them in your claypot. They soon cook down and make an excellent light accompaniment to broiled delicate fish such as salmon or trout.

❖

1 small iceberg lettuce, quartered
2 small radicchio lettuces, halved
2 heads Belgian endive, halved
1 Tbsp olive oil
2 Tbsp lemon juice
½ tsp finely grated lemon rind
1 tsp wholegrain mustard
1 tsp clear honey
salt and black pepper
1 small bunch basil leaves, shredded
thin strips of lemon rind, to garnish

❖

PREPARATION TIME / 5 MINUTES
COOKING TIME / 25 MINUTES
serves 4

Presoak the claypot as directed and line the bottom with waxed paper. Rinse the lettuces and endive under cold running water to flush out any trapped earth. Shake carefully to remove excess water and then pat dry using paper towels. Place in the prepared pot.

In a small jug, mix together the oil, lemon juice and rind, mustard, honey, and seasoning. Pour over the lettuces and endive. Cover and place in a cold oven. Set the oven to 450° and cook for 25 minutes until tender.

Transfer to warmed serving plates and sprinkle with the shredded basil. Spoon over the cooking juices and garnish with lemon rind before serving.

NUTRITION FACTS	
Serving size 1 (73g)	
Calories 48	Calories from fat 36
	% daily value*
Total fat 4g	5%
Saturated fat 0g	2%
Cholesterol 0mg	0%
Sodium 170mg	7%
Total carbohydrate 4g	1%
Dietary fiber 1g	6%
Sugars 3g	0%
Protein 1g	0%
*Percent daily values are based on a 2,000-calorie diet	

eggplant parmigiana

Eggplant is a member of the tomato family. It has a spongy texture and is quite watery. Salt this vegetable before using to remove any bitterness and to reduce its water content.

❈

2 large eggplants

4 Tbsp salt

two 14-oz cans chopped tomatoes

4 Tbsp tomato paste

1 tsp dried oregano

2 tsp superfine sugar

black pepper

1 large onion, peeled and chopped

2 garlic cloves, peeled and minced

one 4-oz piece low-fat mozzarella cheese, sliced

4 Tbsp dry white breadcrumbs

2 Tbsp freshly grated Parmesan cheese

oregano leaves, to garnish

❈

PREPARATION TIME / 10 MINUTES PLUS SOAKING

COOKING TIME / 1 HOUR 20 MINUTES

serves 4

Trim the eggplants and cut into ½-inch thick slices. Layer in a large mixing bowl with salt and set aside for 30 minutes. Rinse well under cold running water, making sure you wash off all the salt. Drain well and pat dry on paper towels.

Meanwhile, soak the claypot as directed. Mix together the chopped tomatoes, tomato paste, oregano, sugar, and black pepper.

Arrange the eggplant slices in layers in the pot and sprinkle with the onion and garlic. Spoon over the tomato sauce. Cover and place in a cold oven. Set the oven to 425° and cook for 1 hour.

Arrange the mozzarella slices over the tomato sauce. Sprinkle with the breadcrumbs and grated Parmesan cheese. Cook, uncovered, for a further 15–20 minutes until lightly golden, bubbling and tender. Serve from the pot, garnished with oregano.

NUTRITION FACTS	
Serving size 1 (378g)	
Calories 189	Calories from fat 36
	% daily value*
Total fat 4g	6%
Saturated fat 2g	10%
Cholesterol 10mg	3%
Sodium 7449mg	310%
Total carbohydrate 27g	9%
Dietary fiber 6g	22%
Sugars 11g	0%
Protein 16g	0%
*Percent daily values are based on a 2,000-calorie diet	

mushroom crumble

This is a substantial dish, packed full of the earthy, nutty flavors of mushrooms. Firmer varieties of mushroom work better in this dish such as button, shiitake, open cap, and flat.

❈

1½ lb assorted firm mushrooms

1 cup shallots, peeled and shredded

1 Tbsp fresh thyme or 1 tsp dried

salt and black pepper

½ cup fresh vegetable broth

2½ Tbsp cornstarch

1½ cups skim milk

for the topping

¼ cup wholewheat flour

¼ cup rolled oats

¼ cup chopped mixed nuts

¼ cup butter or margarine, softened

2 Tbsp fresh chives, chopped

❈

PREPARATION TIME / 10 MINUTES

COOKING TIME / 1 HOUR

serves 4

Presoak the claypot as directed. Wipe the mushrooms. Halve button mushrooms, quarter open cap and *shiitake*, and slice flat mushrooms, if using, Place in the pot and stir in the shallots, thyme, seasoning, and broth.

Cover and place in a cold oven. Set oven to 425° and cook for 40 minutes, stirring occasionally, until tender.

Twenty minutes before the end of cooking place the cornstarch in a saucepan, and blend in a little of the milk to form a paste. Pour in the remaining milk and heat, stirring until thick. Set aside.

Prepare the topping. Mix together the flour, rolled oats, and mixed nuts. Using a fork, mix in the butter or margarine until the mixture resembles coarse bread crumbs. Stir in the chives and season well.

When the mushrooms are cooked, carefully drain the cooking liquid into the prepared sauce, and whisk until smooth. Stir into the pot to incorporate the mushrooms. Sprinkle over the topping and return to the oven. Cook, uncovered, for a further 15 to 20 minutes, until golden.

NUTRITION FACTS	
Serving size 1 (299g)	
Calories 196	Calories from fat 54
	% daily value*
Total fat 6g	9%
Saturated fat 1g	5%
Cholesterol 2mg	1%
Sodium 642mg	27%
Total carbohydrate 28g	9%
Dietary fiber 5g	19%
Sugars 8g	0%
Protein 11g	0%
*Percent daily values are based on a 2,000-calorie diet	

vegetable lasagne

Lasagne can be a complicated dish to assemble and cook; it is usually very rich and high in calories. This recipe is much simpler, very tasty, and is low in fat as well.

❖

1 large onion, peeled and chopped
1 garlic clove, peeled and minced
1 medium red bell pepper, deseeded and sliced
1 medium orange bell pepper, deseeded and sliced
2 medium zucchini, trimmed and sliced
1 medium eggplant, trimmed and diced
two 14-oz cans chopped tomatoes
2 Tbsp tomato paste
1 bouquet garni
salt and black pepper
2 Tbsp cornstarch
2¼ cups skim milk
4 "quick-cook" sheets green lasagne
4 Tbsp freshly grated Parmesan cheese

❖

PREPARATION TIME / 15 MINUTES
COOKING TIME / 1 HOUR 35 MINUTES
serves 4

Presoak the claypot as directed. Place the onions, garlic, bell peppers, zucchini, eggplant, chopped tomatoes, and tomato paste in the pot. Mix well. Push in the bouquet garni and season well. Cover and place in a cold oven. Set the oven to 425° and cook for 1 hour.

Meanwhile, make the white sauce. Blend the cornstarch with a little of the milk and then transfer to a saucepan. Add the remaining milk and heat through, stirring, until thickened. Cover the surface with a piece of plastic wrap to prevent a skin forming and set aside until required.

Lay the lasagne sheets over the vegetables and spoon over the white sauce. Spread over to cover completely. Cover again and cook for a further 20 minutes.

Sprinkle with the cheese and cook, uncovered, for a further 10–15 minutes until lightly golden and tender. Serve straight from the pot.

PICTURED LEFT.

NUTRITION FACTS
Serving size 1 (748g)
Calories 439   Calories from fat 54

	% daily value*
Total fat 6g	9%
Saturated fat 2g	11%
Cholesterol 11mg	4%
Sodium 750mg	31%
Total carbohydrate 78g	26%
Dietary fiber 8g	33%
Sugars 14g	0%
Protein 22g	0%

*Percent daily values are based on a 2,000-calorie diet

curried potato and cauliflower bake

In India this dish is called Aloo Gobi. It is flavored with fragrant spices like cardamom and ginger. Serve this as part of an Indian meal.

❖

1 lb potatoes, peeled and cut into 1-inch cubes
1 medium cauliflower, broken into small florets
6 cardamom pods
4 Tbsp canned coconut milk
1 tsp black mustard seeds
one 1-inch piece ginger root, peeled and grated
1 tsp ground turmeric
1 tsp ground coriander
½ tsp salt
2 Tbsp garbanzo flour or all-purpose flour
1 cup fresh vegetable broth
2 Tbsp chopped cilantro

❖

PREPARATION TIME / 10 MINUTES
COOKING TIME / 1 HOUR 15 MINUTES
serves 4

Presoak the claypot as directed. Place the potatoes and cauliflower in the pot and mix together.

Split open the cardamom pods and scrape out the seeds into a small jug. Mix in the coconut milk, mustard seeds, ginger, turmeric, ground coriander, salt, and flour to form a paste.

Gradually blend in the broth and then pour over the vegetables. Cover and place in a cold oven. Set the oven to 425° and cook for 1 hour 15 minutes until tender. Stand for 10 minutes, before serving, sprinkled with chopped cilantro.

NUTRITION FACTS
Serving size 1 (297g)
Calories 227   Calories from fat 36

	% daily value*
Total fat 4g	7%
Saturated fat 3g	16%
Cholesterol 0mg	0%
Sodium 196mg	8%
Total carbohydrate 42g	14%
Dietary fiber 7g	26%
Sugars 3g	0%
Protein 7g	0%

*Percent daily values are based on a 2,000-calorie diet

maple sweet potatoes and squash

Adding a little maple syrup to these vegetables enhances their natural sweetness. This recipe would also work with white potatoes, and you can use whichever is your favorite squash.

❖

1½ lb sweet potatoes
1½ lb squash such as butternut, acorn or crown prince
4 bay leaves
4 Tbsp maple syrup
2 Tbsp butter
½ tsp ground mace
salt and black pepper
2 Tbsp chopped parsley

❖

PREPARATION TIME / 10 MINUTES
COOKING TIME / 50 MINUTES
serves 4

Presoak a large claypot as directed. Place the potatoes, unpeeled, in a saucepan and cover with water. Bring to a boil and cook for 20–30 minutes, depending on size, until just tender. Drain and set aside until cool enough to handle.

Meanwhile, halve and deseed the squash. Leaving the skin on, cut into 1-inch thick wedges, and place in the pot. Peel the sweet potatoes and cut into ½-inch thick rounds, and arrange in between the squash. Push in the bay leaves.

Place the maple syrup, butter, and mace in a small saucepan, and heat gently to melt. Do not overheat. Cool for 10 minutes then pour over the potatoes and squash. Season well, cover, and place in a cold oven. Set the oven to 425° and cook for 40 minutes. Remove the lid and cook for a further 10 minutes or until tender.

Discard the bay leaves and sprinkle with chopped parsley to serve.

PICTURED RIGHT.

NUTRITION FACTS

Serving size 1 (370g)

Calories 336   Calories from fat 63

	% daily value*
Total fat 7g	11%
Saturated fat 4g	20%
Cholesterol 16mg	5%
Sodium 229mg	10%
Total carbohydrate 67g	22%
Dietary fiber 9g	38%
Sugars 31g	0%
Protein 4g	0%

*Percent daily values are based on a 2,000-calorie diet

clay roasted herb and garlic new potatoes

This recipe makes a change from boiled new potatoes and this method of cooking them brings out their natural sweetness. Choose roughly same size potatoes for even cooking.

❖

2 lb baby new potatoes, scrubbed
4 garlic cloves, peeled and finely sliced
4 Tbsp assorted mixed herbs or 1 Tbsp dried mixed herbs
4 Tbsp fresh vegetable broth
black pepper
2 tsp coarse sea salt

❖

PREPARATION TIME / 5 MINUTES
COOKING TIME / 1 HOUR 15 MINUTES
serves 4

Presoak the claypot as directed. Place the potatoes in the pot, and push the garlic cloves in between the potatoes.

Sprinkle with the herbs and spoon over the broth. Season with pepper. Cover and place in a cold oven. Set oven to 400° and cook for 1 hour, turning the potatoes occasionally.

Remove the lid, sprinkle with the salt and cook, uncovered, for a further 15 minutes, until lightly golden and crisp.

NUTRITION FACTS

Serving size 1 (297g)

Calories 125   Calories from fat 0

	% daily value*
Total fat 0g	0%
Saturated fat 0g	0%
Cholesterol 0mg	0%
Sodium 960mg	40%
Total carbohydrate 29g	10%
Dietary fiber 2g	8%
Sugars 0g	0%
Protein 2g	0%

*Percent daily values are based on a 2,000-calorie diet

vegetable mélange

This colorful dish of assorted vegetables, cooked very simply and flavored with thyme, will brighten up any meal. You can use any combination of vegetables, so long as they require the same cooking time.

2 butternut squash
1 large zucchini
1 large red bell pepper, deseeded and sliced into rings
1 large yellow bell pepper, deseeded and sliced into rings
1 medium red onion, peeled and sliced
8 oz large open cup mushrooms, wiped and halved
1 Tbsp lemon juice
1 Tbsp olive oil
1 Tbsp chopped fresh thyme or 1 tsp dried
salt and black pepper
sprigs of thyme, to garnish

PREPARATION TIME / 10 MINUTES
COOKING TIME / 1 HOUR
serves 4

Presoak the claypot as directed. Using a sharp knife, peel off the skin from the squash. Halve widthways and scoop out the seeds. Cut each into eight equal wedges, and place in the pot.

Wash and trim the zucchini and cut into five thick strips, and add to the pot along with the bell peppers, onion, and mushrooms. Mix together the lemon juice, oil, and thyme, and pour over the vegetables. Mix well and season generously.

Cover and place in a cold oven. Set the oven to 425° and cook for 45 minutes. Remove the lid and cook for a further 15 minutes or until tender and lightly charred.

PICTURED LEFT.

NUTRITION FACTS

Serving size 1 (225g)

Calories 75   Calories from fat 36

	% daily value*
Total fat 4g	6%
Saturated fat 1g	3%
Cholesterol 0mg	0%
Sodium 151mg	6%
Total carbohydrate 10g	4%
Dietary fiber 3g	11%
Sugars 4g	0%
Protein 2g	0%

*Percent daily values are based on a 2,000-calorie diet

mushroom cannelloni

Cannelloni is traditionally a rich dish of meat-stuffed pasta tubes baked in a rich tomato sauce with lashings of cheese. This much lighter version uses mushrooms as a substitute, and tastes equally delicious.

10 oz mixed mushrooms such as button, open cup, shiitake or chanterelle, wiped
1 medium onion, peeled and roughly chopped
½ tsp ground nutmeg
½ cup low-fat soft cheese flavored with garlic and herbs
4 Tbsp dry white wine
3 Tbsp fresh white breadcrumbs
salt and black pepper
12 dried "quick-cook" cannelloni tubes

for the sauce

1 cup dry white wine
1 cup puréed tomatoes
2 Tbsp tomato paste
1 tsp superfine sugar
2 bay leaves

to serve

1 small bunch basil leaves, shredded
one 1-oz piece Parmesan cheese

PREPARATION TIME / 20 MINUTES
COOKING TIME / 55 MINUTES
serves 4

Presoak the claypot as directed and line the base with waxed paper. Place the cannelloni ingredients, except the tubes, in a blender and blend for a few seconds until well chopped. Alternatively, finely chop the mushrooms and onion by hand and mix with the other ingredients.

Using a teaspoon, fill each tube with a little of the mushroom mixture and place the tubes in the pot.

Mix all the sauce ingredients together and season well. Pour over the pasta tubes, making sure they are completely covered. Cover with the lid and place in a cold oven. Set the oven to 425° and bake for 40 minutes. Remove the lid and cook for a further 10–15 minutes until tender.

Discard the bay leaves and sprinkle with the shredded basil. Using a vegetable peeler, shave off pieces of cheese onto the cannelloni and serve.

NUTRITION FACTS

Serving size 1 (375g)

Calories 520   Calories from fat 63

	% daily value*
Total fat 7g	10%
Saturated fat 3g	17%
Cholesterol 14mg	4%
Sodium 349mg	15%
Total carbohydrate 83g	28%
Dietary fiber 5g	20%
Sugars 13g	0%
Protein 17g	0%

*Percent daily values are based on a 2,000-calorie diet

beetroot and potato bake

The strong color of beetroot merges with the potato in this recipe to produce an attractive pink vegetable dish. Serve with roast meats or rich casseroles.

❧

1 lb beetroot, peeled and coarsely grated
1 medium red onion, peeled and shredded
½ tsp ground allspice
2 Tbsp lemon juice
1 Tbsp light brown sugar
salt and black pepper
1½ lb potatoes, peeled and thinly sliced
½ cup fresh vegetable broth
2 tsp caraway seeds
1 Tbsp chopped parsley
½ cup plain yogurt, to serve

❧

PREPARATION TIME / 15 MINUTES
COOKING TIME / 1 HOUR 5 MINUTES
serves 4

Presoak a small claypot as directed and line the bottom with waxed paper. Place the beetroot in a bowl and mix in the onion, allspice, lemon juice, and brown sugar. Season.

Place half the potato in layers at the bottom of the claypot, season, and pile over the beetroot mixture. Top with the remaining potato slices and pour over the broth. Sprinkle with the seeds.

Cover and place in a cold oven. Set the oven to 425°. Cook for 55 minutes. Remove the lid and cook for a further 10 minutes until lightly browned. Serve sprinkled with parsley and accompanied with spoonfuls of yogurt.

PICTURED RIGHT.

NUTRITION FACTS

Serving size 1 (365g)

Calories 278   Calories from fat 9

	% daily value*
Total fat 1g	1%
Saturated fat 0g	0%
Cholesterol 1mg	0%
Sodium 223mg	9%
Total carbohydrate 62g	21%
Dietary fiber 5g	21%
Sugars 7g	0%
Protein 8g	0%

*Percent daily values are based on a 2,000-calorie diet

indian rice with split peas

Although this dish is based around humble ingredients, it is very delicious and is often served as part of an Indian banquet. Serve this with any meat dish, or with a crisp salad and a mint raita.

❧

¼ cup skinned chana dal (yellow split peas)
1¼ cups Basmati rice
½ tsp ground turmeric
2 tsp vegetable oil
1 large onion, peeled and shredded
2 garlic cloves, peeled and minced
one 1-inch piece ginger root, peeled and finely chopped
4 Tbsp plain yogurt
½ tsp salt
2 Tbsp lemon juice
2 Tbsp canned coconut milk
2 fresh green chiles, deseeded and finely chopped
2 tsp garam masala
2 Tbsp chopped cilantro

❧

PREPARATION TIME / 15 MINUTES PLUS SOAKING
COOKING TIME / 1 HOUR 9 MINUTES
serves 6

Presoak the claypot as directed. Wash the chana dal (yellow split peas) in cold running water. Place in a bowl, cover with cold water and soak for 1 hour 30 minutes. Meanwhile, wash the rice, place in another bowl, cover with cold water, and set aside for 30 minutes.

Transfer the soaked dal and liquid to a large saucepan and add the turmeric. Bring to a boil, partially cover, and simmer for 30 minutes until just tender. Drain well and place in a bowl.

Heat the oil in a skillet and gently fry the onion, garlic, ginger, and spices for 3–4 minutes until just softened. Stir into the dal with the yogurt and salt.

Drain the rice, place in a saucepan, and cover with water. Bring to a boil and cook for 5 minutes. Drain and cool for 10 minutes.

Place half the rice in the bottom of the claypot. Spoon over the dal, and top with remaining rice. Sprinkle with lemon juice, coconut, chiles, and garam masala.

Cover and place in a cold oven. Set the oven to 425° and cook for 30 minutes. Sprinkle with the chopped cilantro and stir gently to mix before serving.

NUTRITION FACTS

Serving size 1 (118g)

Calories 212   Calories from fat 45

	% daily value*
Total fat 5g	7%
Saturated fat 1g	7%
Cholesterol 1mg	0%
Sodium 365mg	15%
Total carbohydrate 38g	13%
Dietary fiber 2g	9%
Sugars 1g	0%
Protein 5g	0%

*Percent daily values are based on a 2,000-calorie diet

garlic fan potatoes

If you're looking for a different way to serve potatoes, then try these. Potatoes cook very well in the claypot; they hold their shape well and retain their tender texture. Sprinkle with poppy seeds for extra crunch.

◇

6 medium potatoes
1 Tbsp olive oil
1 garlic clove, peeled and minced
1 tsp dried marjoram
salt and black pepper
1 Tbsp poppy seeds

◇

PREPARATION TIME / 10 MINUTES
COOKING TIME / 1 HOUR 30 MINUTES
serves 6

Presoak the claypot as directed and line the bottom with waxed paper. Peel the potatoes. With a sharp knife, cut each potato crossways into ¼-inch slices, being careful to cut each slice only three-quarters of the way through the potato.

Place the potatoes in the pot. Mix together the oil, garlic, and marjoram. Brush over the potatoes and season well. Cover and place in a cold oven. Set the oven to 400° and cook for about 1 hour, until tender.

Remove the lid, baste with the cooking juices, sprinkle with the poppy seeds, and cook, uncovered, for a further 10–15 minutes until lightly golden. Drain and serve.

NUTRITION FACTS	
Serving size 1 (106g)	
Calories 139	Calories from fat 27
	% daily value*
Total fat 3g	5%
Saturated fat 0g	2%
Cholesterol 0mg	0%
Sodium 105mg	4%
Total carbohydrate 26g	9%
Dietary fiber 3g	11%
Sugars 2g	0%
Protein 3g	0%

*Percent daily values are based on a 2,000-calorie diet

saffron risotto

Risotto is usually made on top of the stove, and involves constant watching and stirring. This claypot version is much easier to make, and the result is just as good.

❖

large pinch of saffron
2 Tbsp boiling water
2 tsp olive oil
1 medium onion, peeled and finely chopped
1½ cups arborio or other risotto rice
1 quart fresh vegetable broth
1 cup frozen peas, thawed
salt and black pepper
¼ cup freshly grated Parmesan cheese
parsley, to garnish

❖

PREPARATION TIME / 10 MINUTES
COOKING TIME / 1 HOUR 10 MINUTES
serves 4

Presoak the claypot as directed. Infuse the saffron in the boiling water for 10 minutes.

Meanwhile, heat the oil in a skillet and gently fry the onion for 3–4 minutes to soften but not brown. Add the rice and continue to cook, stirring, for 2 minutes until the rice is coated in the onion mixture. Cool for 10 minutes.

Transfer the mixture to the pot. Mix the broth and saffron liquid and pour over the rice. Cover and place in a cold oven. Set the oven to 375° and cook for 1 hour to 1 hour 15 minutes until thick and creamy, stirring occasionally.

Stir in the peas and season well. Cook, uncovered, for a further 10 minutes until heated through. Just before serving, stir in the grated cheese and serve garnished with parsley.

NUTRITION FACTS	
Serving size 1 (365g)	
Calories 208 Calories from fat 36	
	% daily value*
Total fat 4g	6%
Saturated fat 1g	7%
Cholesterol 4mg	1%
Sodium 356mg	15%
Total carbohydrate 36g	12%
Dietary fiber 3g	10%
Sugars 3g	0%
Protein 7g	0%
*Percent daily values are based on a 2,000-calorie diet	

chapter **six**

desserts

baked apples and pears in red wine

Fruit cooks particularly well in the claypot. Here the fruits of the fall are baked in red wine sweetened with brown sugar with the added hint of spice. A truly warming dessert, which is equally delicious served cold.

❄

4 medium ripe pears
2 medium apples
1 medium lemon
1 cinnamon stick, broken
6 cloves
2 bay leaves
¼ cup light brown sugar
1 cup dry red wine

❄

PREPARATION TIME / **10 MINUTES**
COOKING TIME / **30–40 MINUTES**
serves 4

Presoak a small claypot as directed. Core and peel the pears and cut into quarters, and place in a bowl. Core and peel the apples and cut into thick wedges. Mix into the pears.

Using a vegetable peeler, pare off four pieces of lemon rind into the bowl. Extract the juice and toss into the fruit along with the cinnamon, cloves, bay leaves, and brown sugar until well coated.

Pile the fruit into the pot and pour over the wine. Cover and place in a cold oven and set the oven to 425˚. Cook for 20 minutes, then stir the mixture. Cover and cook for a further 10–20 minutes, depending on ripeness, until tender.

Discard the spices, lemon rind, and bay leaves before serving with plain yogurt.

NUTRITION FACTS	
Serving size 1 (319g)	
Calories 239	Calories from fat 9
	% daily value*
Total fat 1g	1%
Saturated fat 0g	0%
Cholesterol 0mg	0%
Sodium 13mg	1%
Total carbohydrate 52g	17%
Dietary fiber 6g	25%
Sugars 39g	0%
Protein 1g	0%

*Percent daily values are based on a 2,000-calorie diet

stuffed almond peaches

Choose fresh, ripe peaches or nectarines for this recipe when in season. If not, you can substitute canned ones but make sure they are in natural juice and not sugar syrup. Use amaretti cookies that are made from crushed apricot kernels rather than ground almonds as these are much lower in fat.

❧

4 medium ripe peaches
2 oz amaretti cookies, crushed
2 Tbsp ground almonds
½ tsp finely grated orange rind
2 Tbsp brandy
1 small egg white, lightly beaten
½ cup sweet vermouth
bay leaves and orange zest to decorate

❧

PREPARATION TIME / 5 MINUTES
COOKING TIME / 30 MINUTES
serves 4

Presoak the claypot as directed. Halve the peaches and carefully remove the stone.

Mix together the crushed cookies, ground almonds, orange rind, brandy, and egg white to form a smooth soft paste. Pile a mound of stuffing onto each peach half and transfer to the pot.

Pour in the vermouth, cover, and place in a cold oven. Set the oven to 425° and cook for 20 minutes. Remove the lid and continue to cook for a further 10 minutes until lightly golden and tender. Drain the peaches, garnish, and serve with a little cooking juice spooned over.

PICTURED LEFT.

NUTRITION FACTS	
Serving size 1 (151g)	
Calories 210	Calories from fat 54
	% daily value*
Total fat 6g	9%
Saturated fat 1g	4%
Cholesterol 40mg	13%
Sodium 35mg	1%
Total carbohydrate 20g	7%
Dietary fiber 3g	13%
Sugars 16g	0%
Protein 5g	0%
*Percent daily values are based on a 2,000-calorie diet	

fruit crisp

This is a colorful dessert of assorted berries with a crunchy cornflake and oat topping. You can use whichever berries and currants you like, simply adjust the sweetness accordingly.

❧

1 cup raspberries, washed, thawed if frozen
1 cup strawberries, washed, hulled, and halved
1 cup blackberries, washed, thawed if frozen
1 cup blueberries, washed, thawed if frozen
2 Tbsp light brown sugar
2 tsp vanilla essence
juice of 1 large orange

for the topping

¼ cup butter or margarine
1 Tbsp clear honey
1 tsp ground cinnamon
⅓ cup cornflakes
¼ cup jumbo oats

❧

PREPARATION TIME / 10 MINUTES
COOKING TIME / APPROXIMATELY 40 MINUTES
serves 6

Presoak a small claypot as directed. Place all the fruit in the pot and stir in the sugar, vanilla essence, and orange juice. Cover and place in a cold oven. Set oven to 425° and cook for 30 minutes until tender but not mushy.

Meanwhile, prepare the topping. Melt the butter or margarine with the honey and cinnamon over a low heat until liquid. Remove from the heat and stir in the cornflakes and oats. Set aside.

Spoon the topping over the fruits to evenly cover and return to the oven. Cook, uncovered, for a further 10 minutes until crisp. Serve hot or cold.

NUTRITION FACTS	
Serving size 1 (139g)	
Calories 180	Calories from fat 81
	% daily value*
Total fat 9g	14%
Saturated fat 5g	26%
Cholesterol 22mg	7%
Sodium 91mg	4%
Total carbohydrate 24g	8%
Dietary fiber 4g	18%
Sugars 16g	0%
Protein 2g	0%
*Percent daily values are based on a 2,000-calorie diet	

caribbean pineapple

How many this recipe serves depends on the size of pineapple you are able to use and fit in your claypot. It is a light, refreshing dessert, which is full of flavor. Remove the lid just before the end of cooking to crisp the coconut.

❧

1 medium or large ripe pineapple
4 Tbsp dark rum
1 tsp ground allspice
1 tsp finely grated orange rind
2 Tbsp dark brown sugar
1 Tbsp unsweetened shredded coconut
orange rind to garnish

❧

PREPARATION TIME / 5 MINUTES
COOKING TIME / 30 MINUTES
serves 2-4

Presoak a large claypot as directed. Halve the pineapple and cut in half again. Strip away as many leaves as necessary to enable you to fit the pineapple pieces in the pot. Slice out the central core if it is tough, and place the pieces in the pot.

Sprinkle over the rum. Mix the allspice, orange rind, and sugar together and spoon over the pineapple. Cover and place in a cold oven. Set the oven to 425° and cook for 20 minutes.

Remove the lid, spoon over the cooking juices and sprinkle with the coconut. Continue to cook, uncovered, for a further 10 minutes until the coconut is lightly toasted and the pineapple is tender.

Drain and serve with the cooking juices spooned over. Garnish with orange rind and accompany with plain yogurt.

PICTURED RIGHT.

NUTRITION FACTS

Serving size 1 (187g)
Calories 166   Calories from fat 9

	% daily value*
Total fat 1g	2%
Saturated fat 1g	3%
Cholesterol 0mg	0%
Sodium 11mg	0%
Total carbohydrate 30g	10%
Dietary fiber 2g	9%
Sugars 27g	0%
Protein 1g	0%

*Percent daily values are based on a 2,000-calorie diet

tropical rice pudding

This creamy rice dessert is flavored with sweet spices which gives it a delicious richness without the addition of fat. You can add whatever dried fruit or chopped fresh fruit you like, but firmer textured fruits work the best.

❧

¼ cup short-grain white rice, washed
⅓ cup golden raisins
2 Tbsp light brown sugar
1 vanilla bean
1 cinnamon stick, broken
½ tsp ground nutmeg
2 cups skim milk
½ cup pineapple flesh, cubed
2 Tbsp dark rum (optional)
2 Tbsp toasted flaked coconut
4 Tbsp dried banana chips

❧

PREPARATION TIME / 5 MINUTES PLUS STANDING
COOKING TIME / 1 HOUR 30 MINUTES
serves 4

Presoak the claypot as directed. Place the rice in the pot and mix in the raisins and the sugar.

Using a small sharp knife, split the vanilla bean lengthways to reveal the seeds and add to the rice along with the cinnamon stick and nutmeg.

Pour the milk over the rice. Cover and place in a cold oven. Set the oven to 325° and cook for 1 hour 30 minutes, stirring occasionally, until the pudding is thick and the liquid is absorbed. Stand, covered, for 10 minutes.

Discard the vanilla bean and cinnamon stick. Stir in the pineapple and rum, if using. Serve sprinkled with coconut and banana chips.

NUTRITION FACTS

Serving size 1 (191g)
Calories 229   Calories from fat 63

	% daily value*
Total fat 7g	11%
Saturated fat 5g	24%
Cholesterol 17mg	6%
Sodium 66mg	3%
Total carbohydrate 35g	12%
Dietary fiber 2g	7%
Sugars 24g	0%
Protein 5g	0%

*Percent daily values are based on a 2,000-calorie diet

cranberry and pear dessert

A delicious combination of sharp, ruby-colored cranberries and sweet, juicy pears cooked in cranberry juice, and topped with a light, sweet topping.

❧

4 ripe pears
1 Tbsp lemon juice
1 cup cranberries
½ cup superfine sugar
½ cup cranberry juice

for the topping

1 cup self-rising flour
½ tsp cinnamon
½ tsp nutmeg
4 Tbsp butter
4 Tbsp superfine sugar
½ cup skim milk

❧

PREPARATION TIME / 10 MINUTES
COOKING TIME / 1 HOUR
serves 6

Presoak a small claypot as directed. Core and peel the pears, and cut each into 6 wedges. Toss in the lemon juice to prevent browning.

Place the pears in the pot and mix in the cranberries and ½ cup sugar. Pour over the juice, cover and place in a cold oven. Set the oven to 425° and cook for 40 minutes.

Meanwhile, sift the flour in a bowl and rub in the butter. Stir in four tablespoons sugar, the cinnamon and nutmeg, and add enough milk to form a soft dough.

Press or roll out the dough on a lightly floured surface to a thickness of ¾ inch and stamp out 12 rounds, using a 2-inch round cookie cutter.

Once the fruit is ready, arrange the rounds, overlapping, round the pot, on top of the fruit. Brush with any remaining milk and sprinkle with the remaining sugar. Cook, uncovered, for a further 15–20 minutes until risen and golden.

PICTURED LEFT.

NUTRITION FACTS	
Serving size 1 (236g)	
Calories 393 Calories from fat 144	
	% daily value*
Total fat 16g	25%
Saturated fat 10g	48%
Cholesterol 42mg	14%
Sodium 168mg	7%
Total carbohydrate 62g	21%
Dietary fiber 4g	16%
Sugars 38g	0%
Protein 4g	0%
*Percent daily values are based on a 2,000-calorie diet	

sweet pasta pudding

Pasta may seem an unlikely dessert ingredient, but it is very delicious. Make sure you choose an unflavored pasta. Small shapes, like the soup pasta, farfalline, work the best. Alternatively, cut short lengths of spaghetti and use those instead.

❧

8 oz small pasta shapes, such as farfalline
½ cup superfine sugar
½ tsp grated nutmeg
1 tsp finely grated lemon rind
¼ cup currants
3 cups rich milk
3 medium eggs, beaten
ground nutmeg to dust
lemon rind to decorate

❧

PREPARATION TIME / 5 MINUTES
COOKING TIME / 1 HOUR 45 MINUTES
serves 6

Presoak the claypot as directed. Wash the pasta shapes and place in the pot. Mix in half the sugar, the nutmeg, lemon rind, and currants.

Mix together the milk and eggs and pour over the pasta mixture. Cover and place in a cold oven. Set the oven to 375° and cook for 1½–1¾ hours, stirring occasionally, until the pasta is tender and custard is set.

Remove the lid and sprinkle with the remaining sugar. Return to the oven, raise the setting to 475° and cook for a further 5–10 minutes until the sugar has melted and is bubbling. Serve immediately dusted with nutmeg and decorated with lemon rind.

NUTRITION FACTS	
Serving size 1 (88g)	
Calories 155 Calories from fat 27	
	% daily value*
Total fat 3g	5%
Saturated fat 1g	5%
Cholesterol 102mg	34%
Sodium 34mg	1%
Total carbohydrate 27g	9%
Dietary fiber 0g	1%
Sugars 17g	0%
Protein 5g	0%
*Percent daily values are based on a 2,000-calorie diet	

maple bread pudding

This is a low-fat version of the classic English bread pudding. It has a rich maple flavor and added natural sweetness and color from some chopped dried fruit. Bread pudding is a very filling dessert, so this quantity will go a long way.

❖

8 thick slices white bread, crusts removed and cut into 1-inch cubes
½ cup no-soak dried apricots, chopped
3 Tbsp dried cherries
3 Tbsp dried cranberries
1 Tbsp butter, melted
½ cup maple syrup
4 medium eggs, beaten
1 cup skim milk
1½ tsp vanilla extract

❖

PREPARATION TIME / 5 MINUTES
COOKING TIME / 1 HOUR 15 MINUTES
serves 6-8

Presoak the claypot as directed, line the bottom with waxed paper, and lightly grease the sides of the pot. Place the bread cubes in a large mixing bowl and mix in the dried fruits. Mix together the remaining ingredients and pour over the bread, stirring well at the same time, until all the bread is coated. Pile into the claypot and press down well. Cover and place in a cold oven. Set the oven to 375° and bake for 1 hour.

Remove the lid and continue to cook for a further 15 minutes until lightly golden and a knife inserted in the center comes out clean.

Cut into wedges and serve with extra maple syrup if liked or some low-fat custard.

PICTURED RIGHT.

NUTRITION FACTS	
Serving size 1 (110g)	
Calories 158	Calories from fat 54
	% daily value*
Total fat 6g	9%
Saturated fat 2g	12%
Cholesterol 126mg	42%
Sodium 219mg	9%
Total carbohydrate 19g	6%
Dietary fiber 1g	5%
Sugars 5g	0%
Protein 7g	0%

*Percent daily values are based on a 2,000-calorie diet

spiced dried fruit compote

There are lots of varieties of dried fruits available today ranging from the traditional to the exotic, so you can use whatever combination you prefer. Dried fruits are sweet and rich, so a little goes a long way.

❖

1 lb mixed dried fruits such as figs, apricots, prunes, papaya, mango, cranberries, blueberries, cherries
1 bottle dry red wine
6 cardamom pods, split
1 cinnamon stick, broken
1 small orange
4 Tbsp cognac
2–4 Tbsp clear honey
wedges of fresh orange, to garnish

❖

PREPARATION TIME / 5 MINUTES PLUS OVERNIGHT SOAKING
COOKING TIME / 50 MINUTES
serves 8

Place the fruit in a bowl and pour over the wine. Cover and leave overnight.

The next day, presoak the claypot as directed. Transfer the fruit and wine to the pot and mix in the cardamoms and cinnamon. Using a vegetable peeler, pare off four pieces orange rind into the fruit. Extract the juice and add to the pot. Cover and place in a cold oven. Set the oven to 375° and cook for 45–50 minutes, stirring occasionally, until tender.

Discard the cardamoms, cinnamon, and orange rind. Stir in the cognac and sufficient honey to taste. Garnish and serve hot or cold.

NUTRITION FACTS	
Serving size 1 (128g)	
Calories 138	Calories from fat 0
	% daily value*
Total fat 0g	0%
Saturated fat 0g	0%
Cholesterol 0mg	0%
Sodium 6mg	0%
Total carbohydrate 28g	9%
Dietary fiber 4g	18%
Sugars 46g	0%
Protein 1g	0%

*Percent daily values are based on a 2,000-calorie diet

strawberry and rhubarb dumpling dessert

In this recipe, strawberries and rhubarb are cooked in orange juice and topped with feather-light dumplings.

⌘

1 lb rhubarb, washed, trimmed, and cut into 1-inch pieces
1½ cups small strawberries, washed and hulled
¼ cup superfine sugar
juice of 1 large orange

for the topping

½ cup self-rising flour
½ tsp finely grated orange rind
¼ cup vegetable suet
4–6 Tbsp buttermilk
1 Tbsp superfine sugar

⌘

PREPARATION TIME / 10 MINUTES
COOKING TIME / 1 HOUR
serves 6

Presoak the claypot as directed. Place the rhubarb, strawberries, and sugar in the pot. Mix well and pour over the orange juice. Cover and place in a cold oven. Set the oven to 425° and cook for 40 minutes until the fruit is tender but not mushy.

Meanwhile, 5 minutes before the end of cooking time, sift the flour into a bowl and stir in the orange rind and suet. Bind together with sufficient buttermilk to form a soft but not sticky dough. Divide into 12 rounds and set aside.

At the end of cooking, place the dumplings over the fruit and sprinkle with the sugar. Cook, uncovered, for a further 20 minutes until the dumplings are risen and lightly browned. Serve immediately, accompanied with low-fat custard.

PICTURED LEFT.

NUTRITION FACTS	
Serving size 1 (176g)	
Calories 125	Calories from fat 9
	% daily value*
Total fat 1g	1%
Saturated fat 0g	0%
Cholesterol 0mg	0%
Sodium 20mg	1%
Total carbohydrate 29g	10%
Dietary fiber 3g	13%
Sugars 16g	0%
Protein 3g	0%

*Percent daily values are based on a 2,000-calorie diet

chocolate surprise pudding

This delicious chocolate pudding is a popular choice with children, because it separates during cooking into a rich chocolate sauce at the bottom and a sponge cake on top.

⌘

4 Tbsp butter or margarine, softened
½ cup superfine sugar
2 medium eggs, separated
6 Tbsp self-rising flour
2 tsp cocoa powder
1 Tbsp low-fat drinking chocolate powder
1½ cups rich milk
2 tsp confectioner's sugar

⌘

PREPARATION TIME / 10 MINUTES
COOKING TIME / 50 MINUTES
serves 6

Presoak a small claypot as directed and line the bottom with a piece of waxed paper. Lightly grease the sides of the pot.

In a mixing bowl, cream together the fat and sugar until light and fluffy, then beat in the egg yolks. In another bowl, whisk the egg whites until stiff.

Sift in the flour, cocoa powder, and drinking chocolate powder, and beat well, adding the milk gradually, until well mixed.

Spoon in the egg whites and fold into the mixture. Transfer to the pot. Cover and place in a cold oven. Set the oven to 400° and cook for 50 minutes until the top is set and spongy to the touch. This pudding will separate into a custard layer with a sponge topping. Serve hot, dusted with confectioner's sugar.

NUTRITION FACTS	
Serving size 1 (115g)	
Calories 234	Calories from fat 108
	% daily value*
Total fat 12g	18%
Saturated fat 7g	34%
Cholesterol 94mg	31%
Sodium 141mg	6%
Total carbohydrate 28g	9%
Dietary fiber 0g	1%
Sugars 19g	0%
Protein 5g	0%

*Percent daily values are based on a 2,000-calorie diet

baking

pineapple upside-down cake

A popular and well-known cake, with pineapple embedded in the top. Cakes keep very moist when baked in a claypot. Serve hot or cold.

2 tbsp apricot preserves, softened
3 slices canned pineapple in
natural juice, drained
3–4 candied cherries
1 stick butter, softened
½ cup light brown sugar
2 medium eggs, beaten
½ cup self-rising flour
1 tsp vanilla extract

PREPARATION TIME / 15 MINUTES
COOKING TIME / 1 HOUR
serves 6

Presoak the claypot as directed and line the bottom with a piece of waxed paper, and lightly grease the sides. Thickly brush the paper with apricot preserves.

Cut the pineapple slices into small pieces and arrange in small flower-shaped clusters over the paper. Halve the cherries and place in the center of each flower. Set aside.

Cream together the butter and sugar until light and fluffy. Gradually beat in the eggs with a little flour. Then sift in the remainder. Add the vanilla extract and, using a metal spoon, fold the flour into the creamed mixture.

Carefully spoon on top of the pineapple and gently smooth over the top. Cover and place in a cold oven. Set the oven to 400° and cook for 50 minutes until risen and firm to the touch. Cool for 10 minutes, then carefully turn out and serve pineapple side-up.

NUTRITION FACTS	
Serving size 1 (103g)	
Calories 315 Calories from fat 153	
	% daily value*
Total fat 17g	26%
Saturated fat 10g	50%
Cholesterol 103mg	34%
Sodium 189mg	8%
Total carbohydrate 39g	13%
Dietary fiber 1g	2%
Sugars 28g	0%
Protein 3g	0%

*Percent daily values are based on a 2,000-calorie diet

mediterranean vegetable bread

Several of the ready-made Mediterranean-style loaves in the shops are drizzled with olive oil. This flavorsome bread has all the flavor it needs from juicy broiled vegetables and herbs with only the minimum amount of fat.

❧

1 small red bell pepper
1 small green bell pepper
1 small yellow bell pepper
one 2-oz package sun-dried tomatoes
¼ cup boiling water
2 tsp dried yeast
1 tsp superfine sugar
½ cup lukewarm water
1 lb strong unbleached bread flour
2 tsp dried rosemary
2 Tbsp tomato paste
½ cup plain yogurt
1 Tbsp coarse salt
1 Tbsp olive oil

❧

PREPARATION TIME / 20 MINUTES PLUS RISING
COOKING TIME / 1 HOUR 20 MINUTES
serves 8

Preheat the broiler to a hot setting. Halve and deseed the peppers, and arrange, skin side uppermost, on the broiler rack. Cook for 8–10 minutes until the skin is blistered and charred. Cool for 10 minutes, then peel off the skin and chop the flesh.

Meanwhile, slice the tomatoes into thin strips and place in a small heatproof bowl. Pour over the boiling water and set aside to soak.

In a small jug, place the yeast and sugar and pour over the lukewarm water. Leave aside in a warm place for 10–15 minutes until frothy.

Sift the flour into a bowl and add one teaspoon dried rosemary. Make a well in the center and pour in the yeast mixture. Add the tomato paste, sun-dried tomatoes and their soaking liquid, the chopped peppers, yogurt, and half the salt. Mix well to form a soft dough.

Turn onto a lightly floured surface and knead the dough for 3–4 minutes until smooth and elastic. Place in a floured bowl, loosely cover with plastic wrap, and place in a warm place for about 40 minutes until doubled in size.

Meanwhile, presoak the claypot as directed. Line the bottom with a piece of waxed paper and lightly grease the sides. Knead the dough again and place in the claypot. Press down to cover the bottom evenly.

Using the end of a wooden spoon, press down into the dough in several places to form dimples in the surface. Brush with olive oil and sprinkle with the remaining rosemary and salt. Cover with plastic wrap and leave for 30 minutes in a warm place.

Remove the plastic wrap, cover with the lid, and place in a cold oven. Set the oven to 425° and cook for 1 hour until risen and golden, and it sounds hollow when tapped. Uncover and cook for a further 10 minutes to brown.

Cool for 10 minutes, then remove from the pot and allow to cool on a wire rack. This bread is best served warm.

NUTRITION FACTS	
Serving size 1 (151g)	
Calories 287	Calories from fat 45
	% daily value*
Total fat 5g	8%
Saturated fat 2g	10%
Cholesterol 5mg	2%
Sodium 893mg	37%
Total carbohydrate 53g	18%
Dietary fiber 3g	12%
Sugars 2g	0%
Protein 8g	0%

*Percent daily values are based on a 2,000-calorie diet

cardamom-spiced buns

The flavor of cardamom is strong, fragrant, and sweet. It is a spice used frequently in Indian cookery. The green seed pods should be split to reveal the black seeds which contain all the flavor.

1 tsp dried yeast

½ tsp superfine sugar

½ cup lukewarm skim milk

½ cup unbleached white flour

½ tsp salt

seeds from 3 cardamom pods, lightly crushed

¼ tsp cinnamon

¼ tsp nutmeg

3 Tbsp light brown sugar

½ tsp finely grated lemon rind

1 Tbsp butter

1 small egg, beaten

for the glaze

2 Tbsp skim milk

2 Tbsp superfine sugar

PREPARATION TIME / 15 MINUTES PLUS RISING
COOKING TIME / 35 MINUTES
makes 8

Place the yeast, ½ teaspoon sugar, and half the milk in a jug and set aside somewhere warm for 15 minutes until frothy.

Meanwhile, sift the flour and salt into a large mixing bowl and mix in the cardamom seeds, cinnamon, nutmeg, brown sugar, and lemon rind. Rub in the butter.

Make a well in the center of the dry ingredients, pour in the yeast, the remaining milk, and the egg. Mix together to form a smooth dough.

Turn onto a lightly floured surface and knead until smooth and elastic. Place in a clean bowl, cover with a damp cloth, and leave to rise in a warm place for about an hour or until doubled in size.

Meanwhile, presoak a large claypot as directed and line the bottom with waxed paper. Turn the dough out again and knead for a further 2 minutes. Divide into eight and shape into smooth, round bun shapes. Lay the buns in the base of the pot, cover with a layer of plastic wrap and place in a warm place for about an hour or until doubled in size. Remove the plastic wrap, cover with the lid and place the covered pot in a cold oven and set the oven to 475°. Cook for 35 minutes. Uncover and cook for a further 5 minutes until risen and golden.

Just before the end of cooking, make the glaze. Place the milk and sugar in a small saucepan, bring to a boil, and simmer for 2 minutes. Carefully remove the buns from the pot, split up and place on a wire rack. Brush with the milk/sugar mixture and cool slightly before serving.

NUTRITION FACTS	
Serving size 1 (43g)	
Calories 90	Calories from fat 18
	% daily value*
Total fat 2g	3%
Saturated fat 1g	6%
Cholesterol 24mg	8%
Sodium 179mg	7%
Total carbohydrate 15g	5%
Dietary fiber 0g	1%
Sugars 6g	0%
Protein 2g	0%

*Percent daily values are based on a 2,000-calorie diet

orange brioche

In France, brioches are often served at breakfast. In this recipe, the amount of butter has been cut back to make them more healthful, and the added orange provides a fresh flavor.

❖

1 tsp dried yeast

3 Tbsp superfine sugar

3 Tbsp lukewarm skim milk

1 cup all-purpose flour

pinch of salt

3 medium eggs, beaten

4 Tbsp butter, melted

1½ tsp finely grated orange rind

2 Tbsp chopped candied orange peel

❖

PREPARATION TIME / 15 MINUTES PLUS RISING
COOKING TIME / 30 MINUTES

makes 8

Place the yeast, ½ teaspoon sugar, and the milk in a small jug and leave in a warm place for 15 minutes until frothy.

Sift the flour and salt into a bowl and make a well in the center. Pour in all but two tablespoons of the eggs, melted butter, and the yeast mixture. Add the remaining sugar and orange rind, and mix with an electric mixer with a dough hook for 5–6 minutes until smooth and elastic.

Cover with a clean dish towel and leave in a warm place for about 1 hour or until doubled in size. Meanwhile, presoak the claypot as directed and line the bottom with a piece of waxed paper. Lightly grease the sides. Turn the dough onto a floured surface and knead for 2 minutes, then divide into eight portions and shape into rounds. Arrange the rounds side by side in the base of the pot and brush with the reserved egg. Top each with a little candied orange peel.

Cover with a layer of plastic wrap and leave in a warm place for 45 minutes or until doubled in size. Discard the plastic wrap, cover with the lid, and place in a cold oven. Set the oven to 450° and cook for 20 minutes. Remove the lid and cook for 10 minutes until risen and golden.

Cool for 10 minutes before removing from the pot and transfer to a wire rack. Serve warm.

NUTRITION FACTS	
Serving size 1 (55g)	
Calories 167	Calories from fat 72
	% daily value*
Total fat 8g	12%
Saturated fat 4g	22%
Cholesterol 89mg	30%
Sodium 160mg	7%
Total carbohydrate 20g	7%
Dietary fiber 1g	3%
Sugars 1g	0%
Protein 4g	0%

*Percent daily values are based on a 2,000-calorie diet

cornbread

Native Americans traditionally used only cornmeal when making bread. Today it is mixed with all-purpose flour for a softer texture. Cornbread recipes vary from region to region, but this version is a very simple, basic recipe.

❖

¾ cup cornmeal

½ cup all-purpose flour

1 tsp salt

1 tsp baking powder

1 tsp baking soda

4 Tbsp butter, melted

1 Tbsp lemon juice

2 cups skim milk

2 medium eggs, beaten

1 Tbsp poppy seeds

❖

PREPARATION TIME / 5 MINUTES

COOKING TIME / 1 HOUR 5 MINUTES

serves 8

Presoak a small claypot as directed and line the bottom with waxed paper. Lightly grease the sides of the pot.

Mix together the cornmeal, flour, salt, baking powder, and baking soda. Make a well in the center and pour in the melted butter, lemon juice, milk, and eggs. Beat well to make a smooth, thick batter.

Pour into the pot, sprinkle with the poppy seeds, cover, and place in a cold oven. Set the oven to 450° and cook for 50 minutes. Uncover and cook for a further 10–15 minutes, until golden brown and firm to the touch. A skewer inserted into the center should come out clean when the bread is cooked.

Loosen round the edges using a spatula and allow to cool slightly. This is best served warm, cut into wedges, to accompany stews and soups.

NUTRITION FACTS	
Serving size 1 (106g)	
Calories 174	Calories from fat 72
	% daily value*
Total fat 8g	13%
Saturated fat 4g	22%
Cholesterol 70mg	24%
Sodium 723mg	30%
Total carbohydrate 19g	6%
Dietary fiber 0g	1%
Sugars 3g	0%
Protein 6g	0%

*Percent daily values are based on a 2,000-calorie diet

cheese and onion bread

A delicious teabread made quickly, without using yeast. The recipe is based on a traditional soda-bread method, and is flavored with onion, herbs, and cheese.

❖

¼ cup all-purpose flour

2 tsp baking powder

2 tsp dry mustard

1 tsp salt

2 Tbsp chopped chives

½ cup grated low-fat Cheddar cheese

1 small onion, peeled and finely chopped

4 Tbsp butter

1 cup skim milk

2 medium eggs, beaten

❖

PREPARATION TIME / 10 MINUTES

COOKING TIME / 55 MINUTES

serves 8

Presoak a small claypot as directed. Line the bottom with a piece of waxed paper and lightly grease the sides.

Sift the flour, baking powder, mustard, and salt into a bowl. Stir in the chives, ⅓ cup cheese, and the onion.

Place the butter and milk in a small saucepan and heat gently to melt, but do not allow to boil.

Make a well in the center of the dry ingredients and pour in the milk and eggs. Beat well to mix, then transfer to the pot. Cover the pot and place in a cold oven. Set the oven to 425° and bake for 40 minutes. Remove the lid, sprinkle with the remaining cheese, and bake uncovered for a further 15 minutes until risen, golden, and a skewer inserted in the center comes out clean.

Cool in the pot for 10 minutes and then transfer to a wire rack to cool. Serve warm, cut into wedges.

NUTRITION FACTS	
Serving size 1 (71g)	
Calories 134	Calories from fat 81
	% daily value*
Total fat 9g	14%
Saturated fat 5g	24%
Cholesterol 68mg	23%
Sodium 409mg	17%
Total carbohydrate 6g	2%
Dietary fiber 0g	1%
Sugars 2g	0%
Protein 8g	0%

*Percent daily values are based on a 2,000-calorie diet

brownies

Traditionally, brownies are packed with chocolate and cocoa, but these lower-fat versions are just as flavorsome, and moist.

◁▷

¼ cup unsweetened pitted dates, chopped

¼ cup no-soak dried prunes, chopped

6 Tbsp unsweetened orange juice

4 medium eggs, beaten

1¼ cups dark brown sugar

1 tsp vanilla extract

4 Tbsp low-fat drinking chocolate powder

2 Tbsp cocoa powder

¾ cup all-purpose flour

¼ cup dark chocolate chips

2 tsp confectioner's sugar to dust

◁▷

PREPARATION TIME / 10 MINUTES

COOKING TIME / 1 HOUR 25 MINUTES

makes 12

Place the dates and prunes in a small saucepan and add the orange juice. Bring to a boil, cover, and simmer for 10 minutes until soft. Beat to form a smooth purée. Set aside to cool.

Presoak the claypot as directed. Line the bottom with a piece of waxed paper and lightly grease the sides. Place the cooled purée in a mixing bowl and stir in the eggs, sugar, and vanilla extract. Sift in the drinking chocolate, cocoa, and the flour, and fold in along with the chocolate chips until well incorporated.

Spoon the mixture into the pot and smooth over the top. Cover and place in a cold oven. Set the oven to 400° and bake for 1 hour to 1 hour 15 minutes until risen and firm to the touch and a skewer inserted into the center comes out clean. Cut into 12 squares and leave to cool for 10 minutes, then transfer to a wire rack to cool completely. Dust with confectioner's sugar before serving.

NUTRITION FACTS	
Serving size 1 (75g)	
Calories 201 Calories from fat 27	
	% daily value*
Total fat 3g	5%
Saturated fat 1g	7%
Cholesterol 66mg	22%
Sodium 45mg	2%
Total carbohydrate 42g	14%
Dietary fiber 1g	4%
Sugars 28g	0%
Protein 4g	0%

*Percent daily values are based on a 2,000-calorie diet

chocolate cherry scones

Using low-fat drinking chocolate instead of cocoa powder gives a chocolate flavor without adding too much fat. Dried sour cherries are best, but you can use chopped candied cherries if preferred.

◁▷

1 cup self-rising flour

1 tsp baking powder

3 Tbsp low-fat drinking chocolate powder

½ cup dried sour cherries, chopped if large

½ cup low-fat soft cheese

½ cup and 1 Tbsp skim milk

to serve

low-fat soft cheese

cherry preserves

◁▷

PREPARATION TIME / 10 MINUTES

COOKING TIME / 30 MINUTES

makes 8

Presoak the claypot as directed and line the bottom with a piece of waxed paper. Sift the flour and baking powder into a bowl and stir in the chocolate powder and cherries. Add the soft cheese and rub in until the mixture resembles breadcrumbs. Bind together with ½ cup milk. Turn onto a lightly floured surface and knead gently until smooth.

Divide the dough into eight and form each into a smooth, round bun shape. Place side by side in the pot, brush with the remaining milk, cover, and place in a cold oven. Set the oven to 425° and cook for 20 minutes. Remove the lid and cook for a further 10 minutes until risen and golden. Transfer to a wire rack to cool and serve filled with low-fat soft cheese and cherry preserves.

NUTRITION FACTS	
Serving size 1 (70g)	
Calories 151 Calories from fat 27	
	% daily value*
Total fat 3g	4%
Saturated fat 2g	9%
Cholesterol 8mg	3%
Sodium 90mg	4%
Total carbohydrate 26g	9%
Dietary fiber 1g	3%
Sugars 13g	0%
Protein 4g	0%

*Percent daily values are based on a 2,000-calorie diet

cranberry and raisin spirals

You can use any dried fruit to fill these cakes, but make sure the pieces are small. Here, dried cranberries and raisins make an interesting combination.

❖

1½ tsp dried yeast

¼ cup superfine sugar

½ cup lukewarm skim milk

1 cup strong white bread flour

½ tsp salt

1 Tbsp butter, melted

1 small egg, beaten

for the filling

½ cup dried cranberries

½ cup golden raisins

1 tsp cinnamon

1 tsp nutmeg

for the glaze

3 Tbsp superfine sugar

3 Tbsp water

2 Tbsp coarse sugar granules

❖

PREPARATION TIME / 15 MINUTES PLUS RISING
COOKING TIME / 30 MINUTES
makes 8

Place the yeast and ½ teaspoon sugar in a jug and pour over the milk. Leave in a warm place for about 15 minutes until frothy.

Meanwhile, sift the flour and salt into a mixing bowl, and make a well in the center. Pour in the yeasty milk, melted butter, the remaining sugar, and the egg. Mix until smooth.

Turn onto a lightly floured surface and knead until smooth and elastic. Place in a clean bowl, cover loosely, and leave in a warm place for about 1 hour or until doubled in size.

Meanwhile, presoak the claypot as directed. Line the bottom with a piece of waxed paper and lightly grease the sides.

Turn the dough onto a lightly floured surface, knead again for 2 minutes and then press or roll out into a 12 x 9-inch rectangle. Sprinkle over the fruit, cinnamon, and nutmeg, and roll up lengthways like a jelly roll, ending with the join underneath.

Cut into eight equal pieces and place side by side in the pot. Cover with plastic wrap and leave in a warm place for 1 hour or until almost doubled in size. Discard the plastic wrap, cover with the lid, place in a cold oven, and set the oven to 425°. Cook for 20 minutes. Remove the lid and cook for a further 10 minutes until risen and golden.

Meanwhile make the glaze. Dissolve the superfine sugar in the water, bring to a boil and cook for 2 minutes until syrupy.

As soon as the buns are cooked, brush them with the sugar syrup, and sprinkle with the coarse sugar granules. Cool for 10 minutes then transfer to a wire rack to cool completely.

NUTRITION FACTS		
Serving size 1 (113g)		
Calories 177	Calories from fat 18	
		% daily value*
Total fat 2g		4%
Saturated fat 1g		6%
Cholesterol 24mg		8%
Sodium 178mg		7%
Total carbohydrate 37g		12%
Dietary fiber 3g		13%
Sugars 10g		0%
Protein 3g		0%

*Percent daily values are based on a 2,000-calorie diet

pecan fruit loaf

This loaf has a swirled filling of chopped pecan nuts and dried fruits mixed in sticky spicy caramel sauce. If preferred, you can use other varieties of nut and fruit. Serve in thick slices.

2 tsp dried yeast
1 tsp superfine sugar
1 cup lukewarm skim milk
1 lb strong white bread flour
¼ cup light brown sugar
¼ cup corn syrup
1 Tbsp butter
¼ cup pecan nuts, roughly chopped
¼ cup golden raisins
¼ cup dried sour cherries, roughly chopped
1 tsp ground cinnamon
2 tsp confectioner's sugar

PREPARATION TIME / 15 MINUTES PLUS RISING
COOKING TIME / 55 MINUTES
serves 10

Place the yeast, one teaspoon sugar, and half the milk in a jug and stand in a warm place for about 15 minutes until frothy.

Sift the flour into a bowl and make a well in the center. Pour in the remaining milk and the yeast mixture. Mix to form a dough. Turn onto a lightly floured surface and knead for a few minutes until smooth and elastic. Transfer to a clean bowl, cover, and leave in a warm place for about 1 hour until doubled in size.

Meanwhile, presoak a claypot as directed and line the bottom with a piece of waxed paper. Lightly grease the sides.

Place the sugar, syrup, and butter in a saucepan and stir until dissolved and melted. Bring to a boil and cook for 2 minutes. Remove from the heat and stir in the nuts, dried fruit, and cinnamon. Set aside.

Turn the dough out and knead again for 2 minutes, then press or roll into an oval approximately 12 inches long and ½ inch thick. Gently reheat the nut and fruit mixture if hard and then spread over the dough, leaving a 1-inch border. Dampen the edge with a little water and roll up the dough, from the shorter end, pressing the edge down to seal well.

Place in the pot, cover with a layer of plastic wrap, and leave in a warm place for about 1 hour until doubled in size.

Remove the plastic wrap, cover with the lid, and place in a cold oven. Set the oven to 450°. Cook for 45 minutes then remove the lid and cook for a further 10 minutes until risen, golden, and hollow-sounding when tapped lightly. Cool for 10 minutes then transfer to a wire rack to cool. Dust with confectioner's sugar before serving.

NUTRITION FACTS		
Serving size 1 (96g)		
Calories 276	Calories from fat 36	
		% daily value*
Total fat 4g		5%
Saturated fat 1g		5%
Cholesterol 4mg		1%
Sodium 52mg		2%
Total carbohydrate 55g		18%
Dietary fiber 2g		8%
Sugars 12g		0%
Protein 7g		0%
*Percent daily values are based on a 2,000-calorie diet		

index